Simply Sartre

Simply Sartre

DAVID DETMER

SIMPLY CHARLY
NEW YORK

Copyright © 2020 by David Detmer

Cover Illustration by José Ramos
Cover Design by Scarlett Rugers

All rights reserved. No part of this publication may be reproduced, distributed, or transmitted in any form or by any means, including photocopying, recording, or other electronic or mechanical methods, without the prior written permission of the publisher, except in the case of brief quotations embodied in critical reviews and certain other noncommercial uses permitted by copyright law. For permission requests, write to the publisher at the address below.

permissions@simplycharly.com

ISBN: 978-1-943657-42-1

Brought to you by http://simplycharly.com

Contents

Praise for *Simply Sartre*	vii
Other *Great Lives*	ix
Series Editor's Foreword	x
Preface	xi
Acknowledgements	xiv
Abbreviations	xv
1. A Full, Varied, and Highly Unusual Life	1
2. Responsibility	15
3. Consciousness	37
4. Freedom	65
5. Sartre's Legacy	88
Suggested Reading	95
About the Author	139
A Word from the Publisher	140

Praise for *Simply Sartre*

"This is a delightful introduction to the life and ideas of Jean-Paul Sartre. Detmer's writing is clear, engaging, and fun to read. The book weaves together accurate overviews of Sartre's main ideas with convincing reasons these ideas are still relevant today. The book ends with useful summaries of 50 of Sartre's works—a perfect roadmap for anyone who wishes to read Sartre himself. If I had to recommend one book to a friend, colleague, or family member on Jean-Paul Sartre, this would be it."
 —**Joshua Tepley, Associate Professor of Philosophy, Saint Anselm College**

"David Detmer's new book will stimulate first-time readers of Sartre, challenge advanced students, and offer political activists as well as scholars much to think about. It demonstrates the clarity of a first-rate teacher and the awareness of Sartre's relevance by someone keenly involved in today's world. Detmer shows a deep understanding of the whole range of Sartre's work, how that work connects with other trends of philosophy, and a fine writer's ability to tell a good story—all in a short introduction."
 —**Ronald Aronson, author of *Jean-Paul Sartre: Philosophy in the World* and Distinguished Professor Emeritus of the History of Ideas at Wayne State University**

"The task of introducing Sartre is challenging and doing so for a short book is daunting. Detmer triumphs, revealing himself as a premier teacher of Sartre's life and philosophy. This accessible and accurate introduction captures how a bookish child became one of the most prominent intellectuals on the twentieth-century world stage and created a legacy that continues to grow well into the twenty-first century. Additionally, with chapters on responsibility, consciousness, and freedom, this introduction conveys the importance and magnetism of Sartre's philosophy."

–**Damon Boria, Associate Professor of Philosophy at Franciscan Missionaries of Our Lady University**

"As a community college professor, I have longed to integrate Sartre's philosophy into the introductory courses I teach, but have struggled to find a good way to do so. *Simply Sartre* solves the problem all the way around: Here we have a brief, comprehensive, and truly engaging introduction to Sartre's alternative takes on issues including the nature of morality, free will and determinism, and the metaphysics of mind and body. Furthermore, it also will require students to consider Sartrean thinking on anti-black racism, sexism, and other forms of oppression. This book is a gift to all instructors who see the value of getting students to take Sartre seriously."

–**Chris McCord, Professor of Philosophy, Kirkwood Community College**

Other *Great Lives*

Simply Austen by Joan Klingel Ray
Simply Beckett by Katherine Weiss
Simply Beethoven by Leon Plantinga
Simply Chekhov by Carol Apollonio
Simply Chomsky by Raphael Salkie
Simply Chopin by William Smialek
Simply Darwin by Michael Ruse
Simply Descartes by Kurt Smith
Simply Dickens by Paul Schlicke
Simply Dirac by Helge Kragh
Simply Einstein by Jimena Canales
Simply Eliot by Joseph Maddrey
Simply Euler by Robert E. Bradley
Simply Faulkner by Philip Weinstein
Simply Fitzgerald by Kim Moreland
Simply Freud by Stephen Frosh
Simply Gödel by Richard Tieszen
Simply Hegel by Robert L. Wicks
Simply Hitchcock by David Sterritt
Simply Joyce by Margot Norris
Simply Machiavelli by Robert Fredona
Simply Napoleon by J. David Markham & Matthew Zarzeczny
Simply Nietzsche by Peter Kail
Simply Proust by Jack Jordan
Simply Riemann by Jeremy Gray
Simply Tolstoy by Donna Tussing Orwin
Simply Stravinsky by Pieter van den Toorn
Simply Turing by Michael Olinick
Simply Wagner by Thomas S. Grey
Simply Wittgenstein by James C. Klagge

Series Editor's Foreword

Simply Charly's "Great Lives" series offers brief but authoritative introductions to the world's most influential people–scientists, artists, writers, economists, and other historical figures whose contributions have had a meaningful and enduring impact on our society.

Each book provides an illuminating look at the works, ideas, personal lives, and the legacies these individuals left behind, also shedding light on the thought processes, specific events, and experiences that led these remarkable people to their groundbreaking discoveries or other achievements. Additionally, every volume explores various challenges they had to face and overcome to make history in their respective fields, as well as the little-known character traits, quirks, strengths, and frailties, myths, and controversies that sometimes surrounded these personalities.

Our authors are prominent scholars and other top experts who have dedicated their careers to exploring each facet of their subjects' work and personal lives.

Unlike many other works that are merely descriptions of the major milestones in a person's life, the "Great Lives" series goes above and beyond the standard format and content. It brings substance, depth, and clarity to the sometimes-complex lives and works of history's most powerful and influential people.

We hope that by exploring this series, readers will not only gain new knowledge and understanding of what drove these geniuses, but also find inspiration for their own lives. Isn't this what a great book is supposed to do?

Charles Carlini, Simply Charly
New York City

Preface

Jean-Paul Sartre was, perhaps, both the most celebrated, and the most hated writer of the 20th century. On the one hand, no other philosopher of the period was more famous, more widely read and studied, more influential, or more honored (he was awarded, but rejected, the Nobel Prize in literature; and 50,000 people turned out for his funeral). But, on the other hand, he was regularly vilified for political reasons by both the left and right; the Catholic Church placed all of his works on its "Index" of works that Catholics, on pain of ex-communication, were forbidden to read; several countries officially prohibited performances of his plays; his apartment was twice bombed (and the office of the journal he co-founded was also bombed); and war veterans once marched through the streets of Paris chanting, "Shoot Sartre!" This book tells the story of the life and work of this extraordinary philosopher, novelist, playwright, biographer, literary critic, journalist, public intellectual, and political activist, focusing on the contemporary relevance of his ideas, which maintain their power to inspire, entertain, enlighten, and enrage.

Indeed, showing that Sartre's work continues to speak to contemporary concerns is one of the primary aims of this book. For while no one can deny the importance of his writings from the standpoint of intellectual history (the experience of the French during World War II and its aftermath can scarcely be understood except by reference to them), some contend that the undoubted power and influence of his work in the 1940s and 1950s is entirely attributable to the fact that it was extraordinarily attuned to the circumstances of the time and place in which it was produced. On this view, Sartre's thought belongs in a museum of superseded ideas—ideas that can be safely ignored as we attempt to navigate the problems confronting us in the 21st century.

I attempt to counter this perception by discussing three key ideas—responsibility, consciousness, and freedom—about which

Sartre advances powerful ideas that are both frequently misunderstood and highly relevant to contemporary situations. In order to provide a context for that discussion, I begin with a brief account of Sartre's life. Aside from its intrinsic interest, Sartre's life, for all its faults, is instructive in that it stands as an example of intense, sustained engagement with certain core ideas over an extended period, spanning a wide variety of activities—most notably philosophy, literature, and political activism. For despite all the changes one can identify in charting Sartre's intellectual development, his concern for understanding and describing responsibility, consciousness, and freedom remains constant throughout his many and varied writings, just as his diverse political stances and activities, however else they may differ from one another, can still be regarded as a unity insofar as they are informed and motivated by his understanding of these central concepts.

In his analysis of responsibility, Sartre develops several of the themes that are now most closely associated with the postwar existentialist movement, such as the idea that we are as much responsible for our omissions as for our acts, and that responsibility cannot legitimately be evaded by passively following the dictates of one's religion, or society, or employer. Not as well known, in part because these aspects of his thought are developed most prominently only in posthumously published works, are his ideas on the importance of truth and freedom, understood in terms of their relation to responsibility, in the development of an approach to ethics that would differ significantly from any contenders that currently dominate the landscape of ethical theory in the western world. While many who read Sartre's works today may assume that his seemingly extreme stance on responsibility makes little sense outside of the context of something like the French resistance to Nazism (in which one's day-to-day choices bring life-and-death consequences), it is my burden in this chapter to argue that Sartre's understanding of this issue applies with equal or greater force to those of us who live in more comfortable circumstances.

The contemporary relevance of Sartre's work on the nature of consciousness, by contrast, is largely attributable to the fact that consciousness has, until quite recently, been an unjustly neglected topic. Because of its seemingly subjective, non-measurable, non-quantifiable quality, philosophers and scientists have historically bypassed investigations of consciousness in favor of inquiries into the more objective and tractable domains of observable behavior and brain activity. But Sartre, as a pioneering phenomenologist (the term will be discussed subsequently), makes full use of his literary talents in undertaking the project of describing the different modalities of conscious experience, including perception, reflection, imagination, memory, and emotion. One of the essential features of conscious experience, on Sartre's account, is that it engages with meanings. Sartre's contribution to the understanding of conscious encounters with various kinds of meaning is important, in part because the philosophical tradition that has dominated the English-speaking world since about 1900 has largely neglected this topic in favor of a focus on language. Sartre, by contrast, situates language within the broader and more fundamental domain of meaning.

The discussion of consciousness takes us into the heart of Sartre's famous theory of freedom, as it is Sartre's contention that freedom, necessarily and in principle, is an essential characteristic of consciousness. In elaborating Sartre's account of freedom, and attempting to clear away some of the confusion and misunderstanding that have historically distorted its reception, I present Sartre's reasons for rejecting determinism and compatibilism (two competitor theories), explain his concept of "anguish" and its relation to freedom, clarify his distinction between two senses of "freedom," defend his seemingly outrageous claim that "the slave in chains is as free as his master," and underscore the connection between freedom and one of his other central concerns—responsibility.

David Detmer
Hammond, Indiana

Acknowledgements

I am greatly indebted to my colleagues in the North American Sartre Society. I have been attending the Society's conferences regularly since 1990, and I learn something of importance each and every time. Even more important than this intellectual and scholarly contribution, the enthusiasm for Sartre that is evident in their conference presentations always reinvigorates my own enthusiasm; and the generosity with which they treat my work, even when they are to some extent critical of it, gives me renewed confidence every time I take up a new project in Sartre scholarship. I refrain from individually naming these friends and colleagues only because (a) listing them would add unduly to the length of this book, and (b) I do not wish to commit an injustice by inconsistently acknowledging only some while failing to recall others whose contributions have been equally important.

I would also like to thank Charles Carlini, both for inviting me to undertake this project, and for his helpful suggestions and comments on an earlier draft of this book.

Finally, my biggest thanks, and love, go to Kerri and Arlo, who inspire me, make me proud, and make my life fun on a daily basis.

Abbreviations

The following abbreviations have been used for works cited in the body of the text. In some cases, I have made slight modifications to the translations of quoted passages.

Works by Sartre

(Note: The dates in square brackets are those of the original French publications.)

AHC   "The Artist and His Conscience" [1950], in *Portraits*, trans. Chris Turner (New York: Seagull Books, 2017) [originally published in French as *Situations IV*, 1964].

ALT   *Altona* [1959], trans. Sylvia and George Leeson, in *Altona and Other Plays* (London: Penguin, 1962).

APAR   "Those Who are Confronting Apartheid Should Know They're Not Alone," translator not credited (1966); https://bit.ly/sartre-apar.

ASJ   *Anti-Semite and Jew*, trans. George J. Becker (New York: Schocken Books, 1965) [1946].

AV   "A Victory," included as a "Preface" in Henri Alleg, *The Question*, trans. John Calder (Lincoln: University of Nebraska Press, 2006) [1958].

BN   *Being and Nothingness*, trans. Hazel E. Barnes (New York: Washington Square Press, 1992) [1943].

BO   "Black Orpheus," trans. John MacCombie in WILOE [1948].

CDR   *Critique of Dialectical Reason*, trans. Alan Sheridan-Smith (London: Verso, 1982) [1960].

CE   *Critical Essays*, trans. Chris Turner (New York: Seagull Books, 2010) [originally published in French as *Situations I*, 1947].

CF   "Cartesian Freedom" [1946], in CE.

COS   "A Commentary on *The Stranger*" [1943], in EH.

DGL   *The Devil and the Good Lord* [1951], trans. Kitty Black, in *The Devil and the Good Lord and Two Other Plays* (New York: Vintage, 1960).

DH   *Dirty Hands* [1948], trans. Lionel Abel, in NETOP.

EH   *Existentialism is a Humanism*, trans. Carol Macomber (New Haven, Connecticut: Yale University Press, 2007) [1946].

FOM   "Forgers of Myths" [1946], in *Sartre on Theater*, trans. Frank Jellinek (New York: Pantheon, 1976) [1973].

ICF   "Interview at the Café Flore: 1945," in *The Last Chance*, trans. Craig Vasey (New York: Continuum, 2009) [1945].

ILTM   "Introducing *Les Temps Modernes*" [1945], trans. Jeffrey Mehlman, in Ronald Aronson and Adrian van den Hoven, eds., *We Have Only This Life to Live: The Selected Essays of Jean-Paul Sartre 1939-1975* (New York: New York Review Books, 2013).

IM   *The Imaginary: A Phenomenological Psychology of the Imagination* trans. Jonathan Webber (New York: Routledge, 2004) [1940].

IOAT   "The Itinerary of a Thought" [1969], in *Between Existentialism and Marxism*, trans. John Mathews (New York: Pantheon, 1974) [1972].

ITM   *In the Mesh*, trans. Mervyn Savill (London: Andrew Dakers, 1954) [1948].

LBSM   "A Long, Bitter, Sweet Madness," trans. Anthony Hartley, *Encounter* Vol. 22, No. 6 (June 1964) [1964].

MAR   "Materialism and Revolution" [1955], in *Literary and Philosophical Essays*, trans. Annette Michelson (New York: Collier Books, 1962).

MFMF   "Monsieur François Mauriac and Freedom" [1939], in CE.

MPCE   "A More Precise Characterization of Existentialism" [1944], in Michel Contat and Michel Rybalka, eds., *The Writings of Jean-Paul Sartre, Vol. 2: Selected Prose*, trans. Richard McCleary (Evanston, IL: Northwestern University Press, [1974] [1970].

N   *Nausea*, trans. Robert Baldick (Harmondsworth, Middlesex, England: Penguin, 1965) [1938].

NE   *No Exit* [1944], trans. Stuart Gilbert, in NETOP.

NETOP *No Exit and Three Other Plays* (New York: Vintage, 1955).

NFE   *Notebooks for an Ethics*, trans. David Pellauer (Chicago: University of Chicago Press, 1992) [originally published in French, 1983, but written in 1947-1948].

ROS   "The Republic of Silence" [1944], in *The Aftermath of War*, trans. Chris Turner (New York: Seagull Books, 2008) [originally published in French as *Situations III*, 1949].

ROW   "The Responsibility of the Writer" [1946], trans. Betty Askwith, in Haskell M. Block and Herman Salinger, eds., *The Creative Vision: Modern European Writers On Their Art* (New York: Grove Press, 1960).

SFM   *Search for a Method*, trans. Hazel E. Barnes (New York: Vintage, 1968) [1957]

SG   *Saint Genet*, trans. Bernard Frechtman (New York: Mentor, 1964) [1952].

TAE   *Truth and Existence*, trans. Adrian van den Hoven (Chicago: University of Chicago Press, 1992) [originally published in French, 1989, but written in 1948].

TE   *The Transcendence of the Ego*, trans. Forrest Williams and Robert Kirkpatrick (New York: Noonday Press, 1957) [1937].

W   *Words*, trans. Irene Clephane (Harmondsworth, Middlesex, England: Penguin, 1967) [1964].

WD   *The War Diaries of Jean-Paul Sartre*, trans. Quintin Hoare (New York: Pantheon, 1984) [originally published in French, 1983, but written in 1939-1940].

WIL   "What is Literature?" [1947], trans. Bernard Frechtman, in WILOE.

WILOE   *"What is Literature?" and Other Essays* (Cambridge, MA: Harvard University Press, 1988).

WOTE   "The Wretched of the Earth" [1961], in *Colonialism and Neo-colonialism*, trans. Azzedine Haddour, Steve Brewer, and Terry McWilliams (New York: Routledge, 2001) [1964].

WSR   "The Writer Should Refuse to Let Himself Be Turned into an Institution" [1964], in CR.

Works by Others

A   Simone de Beauvoir, *Adieux: A Farewell to Sartre*, trans. Patrick O'Brian (New York: Pantheon, 1984) [1981].

BR   Bertrand Russell, *The Autobiography of Bertrand Russell: The Final Years: 1944-1969* (New York: Bantam, 1970).

CR   Michel Contat and Michel Rybalka, eds., *The Writings of*

Jean-Paul Sartre, Vol. 1: A Bibliographical Life, trans. Richard McCleary (Evanston, IL: Northwestern University Press, 1974) [1970].

DDS David Detmer, "Dragged Down by the Stone: Pink Floyd, Alienation, and the Pressures of Life," in George A. Reisch, ed., *Pink Floyd and Philosophy* (Chicago: Open Court, 2007).

FJ Fredric Jameson, "Afterword" to Jean-Paul Sartre, *What is Subjectivity?*, trans. David Broder and Trista Selous (New York: Verso, 2016).

GC George Cotkin, *Existential America* (Baltimore: The Johns Hopkins University Press, 2003).

GER John Gerassi, *Jean-Paul Sartre: Hated Conscience of His Century, Vol. 1: Protestant or Protester?* (Chicago: University of Chicago Press, 1989).

GM Robert Atwan, "Great Moments in Literary Baseball," *The Atlantic* (May 1987); https://www.theatlantic.com/magazine/archive/1987/05/great-moments-in-literary-baseball/306167/.

HAY Ronald Hayman, *Sartre: A Life* (New York: Simon and Schuster, 1987).

IPI David Detmer, "Inauthenticity and Personal Identity in Zelig," in Mark T. Conard and Aeon J. Skoble, eds., *Woody Allen and Philosophy* (Chicago: Open Court, 2004).

JB Jean Baudrillard, *Impossible Exchange*, trans. Chris Turner (London: Verso, 2001).

LEAK Andrew Leak, *Jean-Paul Sartre* (London: Reaktion Books, 2006).

PB Patrick Baert, *The Existentialist Moment: The Rise of Sartre as a Public Intellectual* (Malden, MA: Polity Press, 2015).

PF David Detmer, "The Philosopher as Filmmaker," in Peter J.

Bailey and Sam B. Girgus, eds., *A Companion to Woody Allen* (Malden, MA: Wiley-Blackwell, 2013).

RA   Ronald Aronson, "*Meanwhile: Jean-Paul Sartre at 100: Still troubling us today,*" *New York Times* (June 22, 2005); https://nyti.ms/3e2s8gT.

TWS   John Gerassi, *Talking with Sartre* (New Haven, Connecticut: Yale University Press, 2009).

1. A Full, Varied, and Highly Unusual Life

Jean-Paul Sartre was born in Paris on June 21, 1905. He ranks, by some estimates, as "the most written-about twentieth-century author" (LEAK, 8). His is the name most associated with existentialism, the philosophical movement that dominated European intellectual life in the 1940s and 1950s before spreading to the rest of the world in the 1960s and 1970s, occasioned by the translation of his writings into other languages.

So much was his life dominated by the world of books that his autobiography, which covers only his childhood, is titled *Words*. In this work, which is divided into two parts, called "Reading" and "Writing," he declared, "I began my life as I shall no doubt end it: among books" (W, 28). He described his excitement at learning to read, and then his joy at spending his childhood in his grandfather's library: "The library was the world caught in a mirror; it had the world's infinite breadth, its variety and its unpredictability. I set off on incredible adventures. ... I met the universe in books: assimilated, classified, labeled and studied, but still impressive; and I confused the chaos of my experiences through books with the hazardous course of real events" (W, 33-34).

Sartre's enthusiasm for books, and for writing, was to last as long as he did. By the end of his life he had authored: four biographies, one autobiography, at least 15 additional nonfiction books (mostly on philosophical, psychological, and/or political topics), 11 plays, two novels (one of which is a multivolume work), one book of short stories (containing five stories), three screenplays, two volumes of letters, 10 volumes of collected essays, and dozens (perhaps hundreds) of additional articles, reviews, prefaces, introductions, and letters, several hundred published interviews, and more than 50 published lectures and speeches.

Childhood

Sartre's father, Jean-Baptiste, a French naval officer, died from an inflammation of the digestive track (enterocolitis), at the age of 32. Since Jean-Paul was only 15 months old at the time, he never knew his father. Sartre's mother, Anne-Marie Schweitzer, was a first cousin of the famous Nobel laureate, Albert Schweitzer. She was a talented amateur pianist and singer. Her son took up the piano at an early age and enjoyed playing duets with her. Aside from music, however, the two shared few common interests.

Following her husband's death, Anne-Marie left Paris, joining her parents in their home in Meudon, near Paris. Thus, Sartre was raised, from 1906 to 1917, more by his maternal grandparents than by his mother.

His maternal grandfather, Charles Schweitzer (Sartre called him "Karl"), was a language teacher and an author of several nonfiction books, including one on Johann Sebastian Bach. He treated his adult daughter and her son more or less equally, as children. She had a 10 o'clock curfew, and the room that she shared with her son was called "the children's room." So Sartre's relationship to his mother began to resemble one that a younger brother would have with his older sister.

"Poulou," as Jean-Paul was called in his early years, was not subjected to much discipline. His mother for the most part relinquished that role to her father, who indulged and pampered his grandson, whom he proudly regarded as a prodigy. Sartre would later claim that this had affected his character in a beneficial way. Because he did not have to learn obedience, he never developed a desire for power or an urge to exert authority over others.

Perhaps the childhood event that affected Sartre's life most negatively was a cold he caught at age three or four. He developed an eye infection, which eventually caused an exotropia in his right eye–a misalignment in which an eye turns outward. As a result, he was left with only 10 percent vision in that eye. In an effort to disguise the asymmetrical alignment of his eyes, his mother kept his curly hair very long, giving him a rather pretty, and girlish, appearance. Then, when he was about six or seven, his grandfather, without Anne-Marie's knowledge or consent, took Poulou to a barber and had his hair cut short. On Sartre's own account, this revealed his "ugliness." When his mother saw his post-haircut appearance, she retreated behind a closed door and wept audibly.

But Sartre found refuge from all such traumas in his grandfather's library, which contained over 1,000 books. Sartre loved to spend his time there, discovering the world through those books. He learned to read at a very young age, and by the age of seven had read Gustave Flaubert's *Madame Bovary*, as well as works of Voltaire, Victor Hugo, and many other canonical authors. And reading quickly lead to writing, an activity for which he was greatly encouraged by his mother. She made copies of her son's texts, and gave them to all her acquaintances. Her brother also contributed, giving little Poulou a typewriter.

In 1917, Anne-Marie married Joseph Mancy, a civil engineer. She moved out of her parents' home to live in a new house with him in La Rochelle, and Sartre joined them the following year. This was the start of a few unhappy years for him. He did not warm to his new stepfather, and he resented having a rival for his mother's attention and affection. Moreover, he encountered problems at his new school in La Rochelle. He was "different"—small, bookish, and odd-looking, due to exotropia—and, inevitably, bullied as a consequence. He responded by retreating even more into his books and his writing. "I had met my true judges: my contemporaries, my peers, and their indifference condemned me. I never got over being unmasked by them: neither a wonder nor a jellyfish, but a little shrimp that interested no one" (W 84).

In 1920, the family moved back to Paris, and life improved a bit for Sartre during these teenage years. He distinguished himself as a student (he had formerly been indifferent and inconsistent) and he successfully launched his career as a writer, publishing several short fictional pieces in small literary magazines.

Academic achievement at a national level would shortly follow. In August 1924, at the age of 19, Sartre came in seventh in the highly competitive entrance examination for the prestigious École normale supérieure. He studied there from 1924 to 1928, concentrating on philosophy. Among the books he had discovered in his grandfather's library were several classic works of philosophy. Having already resolved to be a writer, he felt that philosophy would be the best thing to study to inform his writing.

At the École normale supérieure he also prepared for the *agrégation*, the competitive national examination for civil service in the French public education system. It qualifies individuals to teach in French high schools and universities. As there are far more applicants than positions available, a national ranking system is used. To the astonishment of everyone who knew him, Sartre failed the exam in 1928—he made a strategic error by concentrating on presenting his own novel ideas, rather than demonstrating his breadth of knowledge. He corrected his mistake the next year and came in first in the nation in the *agrégation de philosophie*. His new love, Simone de Beauvoir, with whom he studied for the exam, came in second.

Simone

If the discovery of the world of books was the first momentous event in Sartre's life, the second was his meeting Simone de Beauvoir in July 1929. She would go on to become one of the most celebrated writers of the century, noted for her novels, essays, autobiographical writings, and works on philosophy, as well as political and social issues. (Her monumental *The Second Sex* is often regarded as the first major work of modern feminism.)

Their love affair, though highly unconventional (they never married, and each, in accordance with an agreement to which they both assented, carried on affairs with several others from time to time), seems to have lasted until the end of his life. In *Adieux: A Farewell* to *Sartre*, Beauvoir's account of the final 10 years of Sartre's life, she wrote, "His death does separate us. My death will not bring us together again. That is how things are. It is in itself splendid that we were able to live our lives in harmony for so long." (A, 127)

An important feature of the Sartre/Beauvoir relationship was that each served as a trusted sounding board, sympathetic critic, and editor for the other. In an interview with journalist and professor John Gerassi, Sartre remarked, "[Beauvoir] made me rewrite hundreds of pages in my life, whole plays. She was the only critic who mattered." (GER 168) And he confirmed this in a published conversation with her: "I had one special reader and that was you. When you said to me, 'I agree; it's all right,' then it was all right. I published the book and I didn't give a damn for the critics. You did me a great service. You gave me a confidence in myself that I shouldn't have had alone." (A, 168)

The Pre-Fame Years

Upon graduating in 1929 from the prestigious École normale supérieure along with Beauvoir, Sartre was required to undergo military service for 18 months. He served in the Meteorological Corps, where he spent a great deal of his time sending up weather balloons.

From 1931 to 1944, with periodic interruptions, he taught in lycées—roughly equivalent to American high schools—in the French provinces. The first interruption occurred during the 1933-1934 academic year, which he spent in Berlin studying phenomenology, a school of philosophy devoted to the study of the nature of conscious experience and of the contents or objects of that experience, that had recently been developed in Germany. During this period he also began his lifelong project of writing and publishing his ideas, bringing out *Imagination: A Psychological Critique* in 1936; *The Transcendence of the Ego* the following year; his first novel, *Nausea*, in 1938;

and two significant works in 1939: *The Emotions: Outline of a Theory* and *The Wall*, a collection of short stories.

The second interruption to his teaching career (but not to his writing) was triggered by Hitler's invasion of Poland on September 1, 1939, which was followed, two days later, by France's declaration of war on Germany. Sartre, an army reservist, was immediately mobilized. He began to fill out his *War Diaries*, which was published posthumously in 1983, and also completed *The Imaginary*, published in 1940.

The Germans captured Sartre on June 21, 1940, his 35th birthday. He was taken at gunpoint to a police barracks and held for several days with little food. In mid-August, he was transferred to a POW camp in Trier, Germany. While there, he wrote his first play, *Bariona*, directing and starring in a performance for the other prisoners at his POW camp.

The Germans released Sartre on medical grounds in March 1941, and he promptly joined the Resistance. There, his main contribution was writing and distributing underground anti-Nazi material. He also resumed his teaching career.

In the early 1940s, he did most of his writing in cafés. He worked simultaneously on his play *The Flies* (which would premiere in 1943), his novels *The Age of Reason* and *The Reprieve* (both of which would appear in 1945), and his philosophical magnum opus, the gargantuan *Being and Nothingness* (which, amazingly, was written in just over one year—it was completed in October 1942 and published the following summer). Similarly, he wrote *No Exit*, by some measures his most successful play, in just two weeks. It premiered in 1944. Sometimes a luminary from the art world—Pablo Picasso, or Alberto Giacometti, or Salvador Dali—would sit in one corner of the café while Sartre worked in another.

In 1944, Sartre and Beauvoir put together an editorial committee for their new journal, *Les Temps modernes* (*Modern Times*), named after the great Charlie Chaplin film. The first issue was published in October 1945. It soon established itself as the leading intellectual journal of the period, and it continues to publish today.

Fame

The mid-1940s was a period of astonishing productivity, during which Sartre, rather suddenly, attained international literary and philosophical fame. His works sold sufficiently to allow him to retire from teaching in 1944 and to support himself solely from the proceeds from his writing. His "reputation developed rapidly. In newspapers and magazines, his face became as familiar—not only in France but throughout the world—as that of any actor or jazz musician." (HAY, 10)

But fame also brought with it relentless and severe criticism. Communists criticized Sartre for his independence, his refusal to join the party, and for his many objections to their version of Marxism. (They were also undoubtedly motivated by jealousy at his fame and influence—he was a rival who offered an alternative to their worldview.) Anti-communists, on the other hand, criticized him for being overly sympathetic to communism. And Christians and cultural conservatives objected to his atheism, bohemian lifestyle, and, in general, his personal and philosophical rejection of the values they held dear.

Increasingly, these criticisms gave way to something more severe: active suppression of his works. In 1946, *No Exit* was banned in Britain; and another play, *Dirty Hands*, was forbidden in Eastern bloc countries for many years. In 1948, the Roman Catholic Church, under the leadership of Pope Pius XII, placed all of Sartre's works on its *Index of Prohibited Books*. (In 1956, Beauvoir's *The Second Sex* and *The Mandarins* were also put on this list of books Catholics were not allowed to read.) Had Sartre's feelings been wounded by this insult—which seems highly unlikely—perhaps he could have taken comfort by noticing the august company he was joining: other philosophers on the list included Thomas Hobbes, Baruch Spinoza, René Descartes, John Locke, Voltaire, David Hume, and Immanuel Kant.

At the height of his fame, Sartre began what would become a lifelong project, that of traveling all over the world and reporting on what he saw. In a trip to America, he witnessed racism firsthand, seeing, for example, two black soldiers refused a table in a dining car. He wrote about it in a June 16, 1945 article for *Le Figaro*. His many travels took him all over Europe, Egypt, Israel, the Soviet Union, China, and Japan, as well as to countries rarely visited by European intellectuals, such as Cuba, Guatemala, Mexico, and Brazil.

Meanwhile, he continued to write and publish at an astonishing rate. Two of his plays, *Morts sans Sépulture* (translated variously as *The Victors* or *Men Without Shadows*) and *The Respectful Prostitute*, premiered in 1946, the same year in which his extensive essay on anti-Semitism, *Anti-Semite and Jew*, was published. His biography of the poet Charles Baudelaire appeared the following year, along with *What is Literature?*, his major work of literary theory. In 1947 and 1948, he filled some notebooks with ideas for the book on ethics he had promised at the conclusion of *Being and Nothingness*. However, dissatisfied with his results, Sartre abandoned the unfinished project. His notes were published, posthumously, as *Notebooks for an Ethics* in 1983. *Dirty Hands* premiered in 1948. The following year featured the publication of *Death in the Soul* (translated variously, and inaccurately, as *Troubled Sleep* or *Iron in the Soul*), the third installment in his *Roads of Freedom* cycle of novels (the first two volumes of which were *The Age of Reason* and *The Reprieve*). *The Devil and the Good Lord*, one of his longest and most important plays, was produced in 1951. And *Saint Genet*, his massive biography of his friend, French writer Jean Genet, the work which illustrates Sartre's theory of "existential psychoanalysis," was published in 1952.

In politics, Sartre attempted throughout the 1940s to forge a "third way" that would be critical of "both sides"–the USSR and the communists on the one hand, and the USA and the bourgeois capitalists on the other. He pursued an anti-Stalinist leftist political path into the early 1950s, at which time he began, increasingly, to align himself with the Soviet Union and the French Communist Party. Sartre's reluctant, grudging support for the USSR in the 1952-1956 period is to be understood partly in the context of, from his point of view, the absence of any viable "third way."

Algeria

But in 1956, Sartre denounced the USSR, condemning its invasion of Hungary—a violent repression of a popular rebellion against Soviet-imposed policies—as a "crime," even though the French Communist Party had defended it. Sartre then resumed his stance as an independent leftist, whose main political concern was anti-colonialism. Indeed, he had started to criticize his country publicly for its colonial rule over Algeria in 1955, prior to the start of the Algerian War of Independence (which the Algerians finally won in 1962). When Les Temps modernes published articles supporting the Algerian cause, the authorities repeatedly confiscated the issues, both in France and in Algeria.

In 1960, Sartre signed the "Manifesto of the 121," an open letter published in the magazine Verité-Liberté. This document castigated the French government for blocking Algerian independence, and the French military for its use of torture. It called for French soldiers to disobey orders and refuse to fight the Algerians. Some of the signatories were imprisoned, and other publications attempting to publish the manifesto were subjected to censorship and/or seizure. In signing the manifesto, Sartre put himself at substantial risk of being tried for treason and possibly imprisoned. But President Charles de Gaulle wisely chose to avoid such a confrontation with France's most famous writer and intellectual, justifying his inaction with the famous quip, "one does not imprison Voltaire."

Other forces in France were less forgiving. A right-wing terrorist group, the Organisation de l'armée secrète (OAS—its slogan was "Algeria is French and will remain so"; it is estimated that the bombings and assassinations it carried out resulted in about 2,000 deaths), placed Sartre's name on their assassination list. In October

1960, thousands of WWII war veterans marched through the streets of Paris chanting "Fusiller Sartre!" ("Shoot Sartre!"). As a result of the OAS's public threat to Sartre's life, for a time no hotel would let him rent a room. In May 1961, an explosion rocked the offices of *Les Temps modernes*. Then, on July 19, 1961, Sartre's apartment was bombed. On January 7, 1962, it was bombed again, destroying both Sartre's apartment and the one above his. Some of his unpublished manuscripts were destroyed in the blast.

Despite these very serious threats to his life, Sartre did not back down. He helped to found the League for Anti-Fascist Movements, continued to make public statements in support of the cause of Algerian independence—denouncing the opponents of this cause as fascists and racists—and marched with Beauvoir in a demonstration supporting the Algerians (the police beat many of the protestors with their batons).

The activities of Sartre and his colleagues in the Algerian cause played a significant role in shifting public opinion in France, thus facilitating the granting of Algerian independence. His exposure and condemnation of the French practice of torture may have helped prevent many from becoming its victims. According to de Gaulle, the Manifesto of the 121 did more to persuade him to grant Algeria its independence than did the constant attacks of the National Liberation Front (FLN)—the political party that spearheaded the nationalist movement in Algeria. (TWS, 283 note 6) Ben Bella, the first president of independent Algeria, when congratulated for the courage and tenacity with which the Algerians had pursued their quest for freedom and independence, replied: "And congratulations to France's intelligentsia, which stimulated that courage and tenacity with its own." (TWS, 298 note 3)

Nobel Prize

But Sartre's increasing commitment to political activism did not put an end to his writing career. A trio of plays, *Kean, Nekrassov*, and *The Condemned of Altona*, appeared in 1954, 1955, and 1959, respectively. These were followed in 1960 by the publication of the massive *Critique of Dialectical Reason*, the one philosophical work of Sartre's rivaling his earlier *Being and Nothingness* in scope, complexity, and importance. And 1964 saw the publication of *Words*, his beautifully written autobiographical account of his childhood.

While Sartre rarely received praise from "respectable," mainstream elements of society for his courageous political activities, he was widely appreciated and recognized for his writing, for which he was offered many honors. But he consistently refused them. He turned down memberships in the ultra-elite, 40-member Académie Française, the Collège de France, and the Légion d'honneur, the highest French order of merit (in this case he was to be honored for his wartime efforts in the French resistance, rather than for his literary accomplishments). Most spectacular and notorious, however, was his refusal of perhaps the single most prestigious international award that any writer might hope to receive–the Nobel Prize in Literature.

On October 16, 1964, having heard rumors that the Nobel Committee–perhaps influenced by the universal worldwide acclaim Sartre's *Words* had received–was considering him for its literature prize, Sartre wrote a letter to the Swedish Academy politely requesting them not to award it to him. The Academy members gave him the prize, anyway. Note that in writing the Academy beforehand, and attempting to decline the award privately, Sartre had tried to spare the Academy the embarrassment of his public refusal. When he declined the award publicly, he was careful to do so as tactfully as possible, as he stated his respect for the Swedish people and for the Academy, and indicated that he had a long-standing policy of refusing official distinctions. The Swedish Academy, for its part, issued a second statement in which it declined to retract the award despite Sartre's decision not to accept it.

Final Years

In the last years of his life, to the extent permitted by his health, Sartre engaged in a variety of activities in support of peace and of the rights of workers, students, and the poor—especially the "wretched of the earth" in Third World countries. In these years, Sartre solidified his reputation among black and Third World intellectuals as the only white Western philosopher who respected them and cared about the injustices they suffered. They recognized him as the first major white philosopher to stand up boldly, forthrightly, and consistently against colonialism and racism.

As a case in point, at a press conference of the French Liaison Committee against Apartheid on November 9, 1966, in Paris, Sartre denounced the apartheid regime in South Africa for its racism and cruelty, and his own government for supporting that regime by selling arms to the South African government (APAR).

Less than a week later, on November 14 and 15, 1966, he was in London for the founding meetings of the "International Tribunal against War Crimes in Vietnam," organized by the celebrated British logician Bertrand Russell. It was Russell himself, perhaps the only philosopher in the world whose fame rivaled Sartre's, who had invited him to participate. In his memoirs, Russell wrote, "I was especially pleased to be joined by Jean-Paul Sartre, for despite our differences on philosophical questions I much admired his courage." (BR, 237) Sartre would go on to be elected executive president of the Tribunal, and to write a moving essay, "On Genocide," presenting some of the Tribunal's findings.

In May 1967, Sartre and Beauvoir rejected an invitation to attend a conference of the Union of Soviet Writers. This was an act of protest over the way Soviet authorities were treating Russian writers and intellectuals, subjecting them to arrest and "reeducation."

Sartre also condemned the August 1968 Soviet invasion of Czechoslovakia—an effort to end the government's liberalization policies known as the "Prague Spring." In October he made a joint statement with Bertrand Russell and another famous and influential philosopher, Herbert Marcuse, denouncing the invasion and demanding an immediate withdrawal of Soviet forces. After the invasion of Czechoslovakia, Sartre made no further trips to the Soviet Union. His "influence contributed—Czech witnesses tell us—to the slackening of oppression during the Prague Spring" (HAY, 17).

In April 1970, Sartre agreed to become the nominal "editor" of a militant newspaper, *La Cause du peuple*. He did so out of principle, even though he disagreed with a substantial portion of the publication's editorial line. The French authorities had regularly seized the paper, and two of its former editors were awaiting trial for subversion. By allowing himself to be named its editor, Sartre, with his fame and Nobel-laureate prestige, offered the paper some measure of protection from such harassment. Either the authorities, fearing bad publicity, would have to leave Sartre and "his" paper alone, or else, should they arrest and try him, the result would be great publicity for the militants and their causes. As it turned out, the authorities did not arrest Sartre (at least at first) but persisted in confiscating copies of the publication from street vendors. Sartre's response was to take to the streets himself to distribute the paper. That did the trick. While he was arrested once, he was detained for only about 90 minutes, and then not bothered again. In response, a right-wing publication, *Minute*, called Sartre "the nation's red cancer," in reference to his leftist leanings.

In 1971, Sartre published the first two volumes of his last major work, *The Family Idiot*, his gigantic biography of the influential 19th-century novelist Gustave Flaubert, one of his predecessors in the pantheon of great French writers. When the third volume made its appearance the following year, it brought the combined page count for the three-volume work to an astonishing total of 2081!

As the 1970s progressed, Sartre's health deteriorated rapidly. Especially devastating was a March 1973 stroke that rendered him virtually blind, and thus unable to write in his accustomed manner. Though he experimented briefly with alternative methods of writing, such as using a tape recorder or dictating to a secretary, he found that they could not accommodate his need to check his work and to make line-by-line corrections, additions, and revisions. Largely as a result of this setback, the hectic pace of his activities slackened significantly in his final years.

But he did not simply retire. In May 1973, just two months after suffering the stroke that robbed him of his ability to write, he started a new journal, *Libération*, which continues to be published today. And he was still capable of significant political achievements. In February 1976, he and Beauvoir organized a petition, ultimately signed by 50 Nobel Prize winners, condemning human rights abuses in the USSR and calling for the release of Soviet dissidents.

Sartre died on April 15, 1980. His funeral took place on April 19 and was attended by a crowd of over 50,000 mourners. He had been, for 35 years, the most celebrated intellectual in France.

2. Responsibility

Sartre's contemporaries recognized the potency of his ideas. While as many readers may have been angered and disgusted by those ideas as were excited and inspired by them, there was no denying that Sartre's message, in its time, struck his readers as powerful, important, and relevant to their lives.

But what is the status of Sartre's philosophy today? To what extent are his ideas relevant to current concerns, or to issues of universal and unending human significance? Some contend that the power of Sartre's philosophy was largely due to its ability to speak to the tense and urgent times in which it was produced—when the French suffered under Nazi occupation, and everyone was forced to confront the unimaginable horrors of World War II.

In response to this contention, I argue that the circumstances in which Sartre first developed and presented his philosophy were not the only ones in which his ideas would be relevant. Rather, they were special because they were among the few circumstances in which that pertinence could be rendered clear and palpable to a wide public. In other words, it is a mistake to think that existentialist principles and issues only matter, or become important, in extreme situations of maximum stress. Rather, they are important in every situation, but this importance tends only to be understood, and to be felt, when the pressure is on, under circumstances of extraordinary strain.

In slack times it is easy, perhaps natural, to take the meaning and value of one's existence for granted, and thus not to raise the fundamental existential questions: "What do I stand for?" "What are my principles?" "What do I consider important?" "How can I give my life meaning?" "To what projects should I devote my time and energy before both are all used up?" Tough times that force one to confront dangers and to make difficult decisions tend to bring such questions to the forefront. But lax times can enable a person to ignore them, sometimes with the tragic result that the person's life is squandered, with their precious time having been frittered away in trivial projects, thoughtlessly pursued, providing neither meaning nor satisfaction.

Sartre's writings shone a bright spotlight on these existential questions. That he quickly attracted readers who readily grasped the urgency of the questions he addressed is indeed partly attributable to the circumstances in which those readers found themselves when first encountering his texts. But it hardly follows, nor is it true, that Sartre's questions are less urgent in our time than they were in his, or that his answers to them are less worthy of consideration now than they were then. If anything, the opposite is true. Since many of us are lucky enough not to have the crucial existential questions shoved in our faces by horrific personal circumstances, we are even more in need of a different kind of stimulus to remind us of the importance of confronting such questions. The enduring value of Sartre's works lies in the fact that they provide such a stimulus and, at least sometimes, help us respond to the great existential questions successfully.

To begin to see this, consider Sartre's short essay "The Republic of Silence," published in September 1944, just one month after the liberation of France. This beautifully written work presents some of his ideas on freedom and responsibility, and explains what it was like to live in France under Nazi occupation:

> We were never more free than during the German occupation. We had lost all our rights, beginning with the right to speak. We were insulted to our faces every day and had to take it in silence. Under one pretext or another, as workers, Jews, or political prisoners, we were deported *en masse*. Everywhere—on billboards, in the cinemas, and in the newspapers—we came up against the vile, insipid picture of ourselves that our oppressors wanted us to accept. Because of all this, we were free. Because the Nazi venom seeped into our very thoughts, every accurate thought was a triumph.

> Because an all-powerful police tried to gag us, every word became precious as a declaration of principle. Because we were hunted down, every one of our acts had the weight of a solemn commitment. The often atrocious circumstances of our struggle made it possible, in a word, for us to live out that unbearable, heart-rending situation known as the human condition without pretense or false shame. Exile, captivity and, especially, death, which in happier times we artfully conceal, became for us the perpetual objects of our concern; we learned that they were not inevitable accidents or even constant, external dangers, but must be regarded as our *lot*, our destiny, the profound source of our human reality. At every instant we lived up to the full sense of that banal little phrase: 'Man is mortal!' And the choice that each of us made of his life and of his being was an authentic choice, since it was made face to face with death, since it could always have been expressed in the form: 'Better dead than…'. The very cruelty of the enemy drove us to the extremities of this condition by forcing us to ask ourselves questions we sidestep in peacetime. All those among us who knew any details concerning the Resistance … asked themselves anxiously, 'If they torture me, shall I be able to hold out?' In this way, the basic question of freedom itself was posed, and we were brought to the verge of the deepest knowledge that human beings can have of themselves. For the secret of a man is not his Oedipus complex or his inferiority complex. It is the limit of his own freedom, his ability to resist torture and death. (ROS, 3-5)

It is clear that this essay's startling first line, "We were never more free than during the German occupation," has to do with *consciousness* of freedom. World War II and the Nazi occupation had made the French people more aware than they were before of their freedom and responsibility, and of the importance of both. Each of their actions could have life-or-death consequences. Since they were constantly subjected to Nazi propaganda, they even had to be vigilant in their thinking, making sure that they were actively and freely thinking for themselves, rather than passively submitting to ideas that the Nazis would impose upon them.

The essay also links the freedom of one individual to that of all of the others. In these extreme circumstances, my actions easily could help or harm others, just as theirs could help or harm me. Thus, freedom is connected to responsibility, reciprocity, equality, and solidarity. The understanding and appreciation of these ideas, which the French achieved by means of their painful experience living under Nazi occupation, also undoubtedly helps to explain the ascendency of Sartrean existentialism in post-World War II France.

But the contemporary relevance of Sartre is revealed in recognizing that the same conditions and principles also apply to us today, and especially to those of us who are privileged to be able to live relatively comfortable lives. Our choices and actions also can, and frequently do, dramatically affect the lives of others. Our decisions are important. It is not as if our world were free of war, violence, poverty, starvation, and oppression. But we tend to ignore the responsibility that comes with our own personal absence of conflict. We face little danger of being imprisoned, tortured, or killed as a result of our actions on behalf of others. We won't be sent to a gulag, concentration camp, or CIA black site. Our barriers to action are not Nazi occupiers, but rather ignorance, apathy, laziness, selfishness, and/or a sense of impotence—the conviction that nothing can be done to overturn the world's horrific evils. We live in a world in which 3.1 million children die of hunger each year. Sartre's message to us would be that we are free to fight this injustice or to accept it, and that we are appropriately held responsible for our choice. In this crucial respect, our times are no different than Sartre's: we, too, confront evils, and are free either to fight them or "collaborate" with them.

Obedience and Conformity

Many people find the obligation to make choices, and then to take responsibility for them, highly burdensome. Such people often attempt to evade this burden by adopting a policy of passively letting others make all the crucial existential and ethical decisions for them. Those who use this strategy tend to think, or at least to tell themselves, that they have no choice but to follow the dictates of, or act in accordance with, the norms and expectations of their culture, nation, religion, and/or employer.

Sartre's argument against this strategy is based on the simple observation that refraining from making a choice is, itself, a choice. This is one of the meanings of his famous claim that we are "condemned to be free." So the commonly adopted practice of thinking as others think, doing what others do, following society's conventions, and passively obeying authorities—whether in government or in one's workplace—is itself a choice, just one option among others. One is still responsible for making it. There is no way to evade the omnipresent burden and responsibility of making choices.

In his famous lecture, *Existentialism is a Humanism*, Sartre illustrated this point by way of an analysis of the biblical story of Abraham and Isaac:

> You know the story: an angel orders Abraham to sacrifice his son.... But any sane person in such a situation may wonder, first, whether it is truly an angel, and second, whether I am really Abraham. What proof do I have? There was once a mad woman suffering from hallucinations who claimed that people were phoning her and giving her orders. The doctor asked her, "But who exactly speaks to you?" She replied, "He says it is God." And what, indeed, could prove to her that it was God? If an angel appears to me, what proof do I have that it is an angel? Or if I hear voices, what proof is there that they come from heaven and not from hell, or from my own subconscious, or some pathological condition? What proof

is there that they are really addressed to me?.... If a voice speaks to me, it is still I myself who must decide whether or not this is the voice of an angel; if I regard a certain course of action as good, it is I who will choose to say that it is good, rather than bad. (EH, 25-26)

For a more contemporary application of this principle, consider the debate in the United States on the issue of same-sex marriage. Those who opposed these unions would often say, "I am not the one who rejects this as immoral; it is God who does so." They failed to acknowledge that it is still they who are responsible for being right about the existence and nature of God, about the correct interpretation of God's edicts, and about the theory that morality is determined by the commands of God.

The Present Paradox of Ethics

Fortunately, not everyone attempts to evade his or her responsibility to make ethical choices. But Sartre pointed out that even those who are most wholeheartedly and clear-sightedly committed to meeting that responsibility must confront a serious difficulty. The problem is that in a world filled, as ours is, with institutionalized structures of injustice and oppression, the urgent need to overturn such structures is often put in direct competition with the equally important obligation to fulfill one's day-to-day duties to family members, friends, colleagues, neighbors, and others with whom one regularly deals. Sartre illustrated this problem with the following, much-discussed example:

> One of my students sought me out under the following circumstances: his father had broken off with his mother and, moreover, was inclined to be a "collaborator." His older brother had been killed in the German offensive of 1940, and this young man, with primitive but noble feelings, wanted

to avenge him. His mother, living alone with him and deeply hurt by the partial betrayal of his father and the death of her oldest son, found her only comfort in him. At the time, the young man had the choice of going to England to join the Free French Forces—which would mean abandoning his mother—or remaining by her side to help her to go on with her life. He realized that his mother lived only for him and that his absence—perhaps his death—would plunge her into utter despair. He also realized that, ultimately, any action he might take on her behalf would provide the concrete benefit of helping her to live, while any action he might take to leave and fight would be of uncertain outcome and could disappear pointlessly like water in sand. ... He was therefore confronted by two totally different modes of action: one concrete and immediate, but directed toward only one individual; the other involving an infinitely vaster group ... yet more ambiguous for that very reason and which could be interrupted before being carried out. And, at the same time, he was vacillating between two kinds of morality: a morality motivated by sympathy and individual devotion, and another morality with a broader scope, but less likely to be fruitful. He had to choose between the two. (EH, 30-31)

Several issues are in play here. One is that no existing ethical theory can plausibly claim to provide the answer to the student's dilemma. The reason is that such theories are necessarily broad and abstract in character, and deal in generalities. As instruments, they are much too blunt to be of much help when dealing with cases in which fundamental values are put into conflict with one another.

It is not that we are unable to achieve genuine knowledge in ethics, for we are able to establish and to grasp such truths as these: that—at least in most circumstances, all else being equal, and in and of themselves, quite apart from their effects—happiness is clearly better than misery, just as health is better than sickness, kindness is better than cruelty, peace is better than war, friendship is better than enmity, knowledge is better than ignorance, intelligence is better than stupidity, honesty is better than lying, and courage is better than cowardice. When we turn our attention away from the ethical controversies that ordinarily attract our attention and instead focus on such banal, everyday value judgments as those just mentioned, it seems clear that we know quite a bit, in general, about what sorts of qualities, character traits, states of affairs, and ways of treating others are good, and what sorts are bad. Indeed, "Everybody knows what good is in the abstract." (ROW, 185) The problem, however, as Sartre noted, is that such general knowledge is insufficient for dealing with some of the tricky situations of life in which one fundamental value is put in conflict with another. Sartre's example illustrates the point that the need to fight injustice (in this case the Nazis) often stands in the way of executing one's other moral duties, so that in a world in which injustice is pervasive, there is a general problem about determining, concretely, how best to carry out one's ethical obligations.

As Sartre's discussion of his student's dilemma unfolded, he invoked Immanuel Kant's great ethical principle, that one should always treat human beings as ends in themselves, and never merely as a means to one's own ends. The idea, roughly, is that only lifeless things should be used as mere means, that is to say, as tools or instruments, items to be manipulated insofar as they can help me to achieve my goals, only to be discarded when they no longer are of use to me. That is an appropriate way to treat, say, a pencil. I simply grab it and use it for writing when it suits me to do so and then throw it away when it is all used up. I do not consider its feelings or wishes, for it has none. But a human being does care how it is treated, and its wishes must be adequately taken into account. More importantly, for Kant, a human being is rational and autonomous, and these characteristics must always be respected. While I will often need the help of others in order to achieve my chosen ends, it would be immoral for me simply to help myself to what I want from them without their consent. Whereas I can simply take a pencil and write with it if I need you to write for me, I will have to ask for your consent to help me, and work out with you—through honest communication, rather than by means of deception or coercion—what the terms of that help might be. You might be willing to help me out of kindness and generosity, or out of friendship, but it could also be in return for payment.

Applying this to the case of his student, Sartre articulated his dilemma (writing in the first person) as follows: "If I stay with my mother, I will treat her as an end, not as a means. But by the same token, I will be treating those who are fighting on my behalf as a means. Conversely, if I join those who are fighting, I will treat them as an end, and, in so doing, risk treating my mother as a means." (EH, 31)

Since Sartre's example addresses the issue of fighting Nazis in World War II, some may take it as further evidence that his thought is dated, and not relevant to our times. But Sartre discussed the same issue in his later writings and made it clear that it arises whenever the fundamental structures of society are oppressive, a condition that is not without application in the present. Perhaps his clearest statement of what he called "the present paradox of ethics" is to be found in his book-length essay, "What is Literature?"

> If I am absorbed in treating a few chosen persons as absolute ends, for example, my wife, my son, my friends, the needy person I happen to come across, if I am bent upon fulfilling all my duties towards them, I shall spend my life doing so; I shall be led to *pass over in silence* the injustices of the age, the class struggle, colonialism, Anti-Semitism, etc., and, finally, to *take advantage of oppression in order to do good*.... But ... if I throw myself into the revolutionary enterprise I risk having no more leisure for personal relations—worse still, of being led by the logic of the action into treating most men, and even my friends, as means.... (WIL, 221-22)

If an ethical concern for family, friends, co-workers, and neighbors prevents individuals from attempting to overturn the economic, political, and social structures of injustice and oppression, perhaps an even greater obstacle is that such a revolutionary project would almost always stand in opposition to the person's interest in faring well in the present.

Examples are easy to produce. If society expects women to confine themselves to a choice among a very small number of possible occupations (teacher, nurse, secretary, or housewife and mother, but not doctor, lawyer, professor, scientist, or business executive), to wear make-up on a daily basis and submit to being judged primarily on their appearance, to defer to men, and to avoid being assertive or aggressive, even in defense of their rights or in pursuit of their most fundamental goals, then a woman in that society faces a choice. She can fight to overturn this system of gender oppression and inequality, in which case she will probably be punished for her nonconformity, or she can play by the current rules, thus standing a good chance of faring well within the limited possibilities available to her, but at the cost of helping to perpetuate society's unjust structures. The same logic applies to the employee who might expose, and refuse to participate in, his company's immoral actions, and risk being fired, or else go along with such actions, and thus increase their chances of receiving raises and promotions. And if Nazis attack your country, you might fight them, or, if you think they will win, you might collaborate with them, so you will be well positioned once they take over. The relevance of Sartre's point lies in the fact that while Nazis are no longer attacking us, the logic of collaboration still is—and it is applied in a thousand different corners of contemporary life.

Omissions

Another way in which many people try to evade their responsibility is by assuming that they are responsible only for their actions, and not for their omissions. But Sartre insisted that the decision not to act is itself, at a higher level of abstraction, an action, just as the choice not to choose is itself also a choice. He insisted that

> one cannot get out of this quandary.... Our very passivity would be an action. The abstention of whoever wanted to devote his life to writing novels about the Hittites would in itself constitute taking a position. The writer is *situated* in his time; every word he utters has reverberations. As does his silence. I hold Flaubert and the Goncourt brothers [French naturalism writers Edmond and Jules] responsible for the repression that followed the Commune because they didn't write a line to prevent it. (ILTM, 132)

Sartre based these conclusions, in part, on what "the occupation taught us" about our responsibilities (ILTM, 132), but it is clear from his reference to Flaubert and the Goncourt brothers that he considers the lessons he learned from the occupation to be valid for other historical periods as well—indeed, for any period in which there are evils which might be either confronted or ignored.

Sartre developed these lessons specifically in connection with the responsibilities of prose-writers, whose "chosen method of action" is "disclosure." (WIL, 37) The role of such writers "is to represent the world and to bear witness to it." (WIL, 230-31) So it "is therefore permissible to ask" a writer this question: "'What aspect of the world do you want to disclose?'" (WIL, 37)

The writer "knows that words ... are 'loaded pistols.' If he speaks, he fires." And if he fires, he must do it like an adult, "by aiming at targets, and not like a child, at random, by shutting his eyes and firing merely for the pleasure of hearing the shot go off." (WIL, 38)

But couldn't one evade this responsibility by simply remaining silent and declining to speak? Sartre's answer is that once a writer has entered the world of writing, "he can never again pretend that he cannot speak." Any subsequent silence must be interpreted as an act—a choice not to speak. Moreover, such silence must be understood as constituting a species of speech: "Silence itself is defined in relationship to words, as the pause in music receives its meaning from the group of notes around it. This silence is a moment of language; being silent is not being dumb; it is to refuse to speak, and therefore to keep on speaking." [WIL, 38] Indeed, there are many contexts in which, as the old cliché has it, "silence speaks volumes."

Thus,

> if a writer has chosen to remain silent on any aspect whatever of the world, or, according to an expression which says just what it means, to *pass over* it in silence, one has the right to ask him [this] question: 'Why have you spoken of this rather than that...?' (WIL, 39).... Why do you want to alter the way in which postage stamps are made rather than the way in which the Jews are treated in an antisemitic country? And the other way around. He must therefore always answer the following questions: What do you want to change? Why this rather than that? (ROW, 170)

And the responsibility of writers is directly related to the responsibility of everyone else, or at least of everyone else who reads. Sartre explained:

> All of us do many things that we should prefer to ignore because we do not want to be responsible for them....
>
> To name one of these actions is to present it, whatever it may be, to its author, saying, "This is what you're doing now; come to grips with it." The deed, thus named, loses its innocence. Language ... brings the person face to face with his responsibilities....
>
> From the moment in which I give a name to my neighbor's conduct, he knows what he does. In addition, he knows that I know it, and in consequence his attitude towards me is changed. He knows that others know it or could know it, and his conduct moves out of the subjective and becomes part of the objective mind. (ROW, 169)

The writer, by naming my misdeeds and by pointing them out to me and to others, makes it more difficult for me to evade my responsibility to correct them. But the same is also true with respect to the misdeeds of others. By calling them to my attention, it is harder than it otherwise would be for me to ignore my obligation to combat them.

Thus, in Sartre's view, the point of writing is "to reveal the world and particularly to reveal man to other men so that the latter may assume full responsibility before the object which has been thus laid bare ... The function of the writer is to act in such a way that nobody can be ignorant of the world and that nobody may say that he is innocent of what it's all about." (WIL, 38)

Truth and Opinion: The Ethics of Belief

But precisely because ignorance of the world's evils provides an excuse for failing to combat them, those who would like to evade their responsibilities often actively court ignorance. As Sartre put it, "The will to ignore is ... the refusal to face our responsibilities." (TAE, 52) He offered an example: "As a bourgeois I want to ignore the proletariat's condition in order to ignore my responsibility for it. As a worker, I may want to ignore this condition because I am in solidarity with it and its unveiling obliges me to take sides. ... Ignorance aims to limit my responsibility in the world. ... Ignoring = denial of responsibilities." (TAE, 52)

Those wishing to avoid having to face up to their responsibilities typically begin by developing a skill at averting their eyes from any area in which unpleasant truths might be found. Thus, for example, the "distinguished carnivore ... refuses to visit the slaughterhouses." (TAE, 34) And a sick woman who is afraid that she might have tuberculosis refuses to see a doctor. That way, since the suspected tuberculosis has not been realized, "there is no obligation to *deal* with it." (TAE, 34)

But the project of avoiding unpleasant truths is both exhausting and dangerous—there is always the possibility that one will accidentally bump into such a truth when one's guard is down. For this reason, the tactic of localized and specific truth-dodging tends to give way to a global rejection of the very idea of truth: "Finally, I hide the very idea of truth. ... I figure quite simply that the truth is not possible. For this reason the sick person who does not want to know that she has tuberculosis will say about doctors: Oh, what do they know! They all have a pet theory, etc. ... The will to ignore the truth turns ... into the denial of truth." (TAE, 41-42)

Sartre concluded that a necessary condition for addressing the world's evils is the adoption of a kind of ethics of belief, according to which it is our duty to seek the truth—an accurate, evidence-based (rather than faith-based) understanding of the human condition, and especially of those economic, political, social, and educational structures that are (1) important to the quality of people's lives, (2) human-created, rather than natural, and (3) capable of being changed for the better. We should also join in the shared project of communicating our findings to others, listening to their reports on their conclusions, and engaging in dialogue with them. The accuracy of these findings might be improved on the basis of helpful comments and criticisms. It is only on the foundation of such a project of knowledge-seeking that the ethical project, that of attempting to change the world for the better, can succeed.

Axiological Freedom Ethics

Though Sartre was never able to construct a fully articulated ethical theory that satisfied him, it is not difficult to determine that his most basic ethical concern is the value of freedom. In the concluding section of *Being and Nothingness*, he asked, "[Is it possible for freedom to take itself for a value as the source of all value ... ?" (BN, 798) While he did not answer that question in *Being and Noth-*

ingness, he did reply in a lecture delivered in 1945, two years after the publication of that book, declaring that "freedom ... can have no other aim but itself," that "freedom" is "the foundation of all values," and that "the ultimate significance of the actions of men of good faith have is the quest of freedom in itself." (EH, 48) And he appears to have maintained this view to the end. In an interview with Simone de Beauvoir, conducted in his final decade (1974), he responded as follows to her question about how he defined "what you call Good and what you call Evil": "Essentially, the Good is that which is useful to human freedom, that which allows it to give their full value to objects it has realized. Evil is that which is harmful to human freedom." (A, 439) Similarly, in another late interview (1971), he declared, "Morality is determined by man's fight against those who limit man's freedom." (TWS, 97)

His most extensive discussion of these ideas is to be found in his abortive *Notebooks for an Ethics*. There, he maintains that "values reveal freedom," and that "any ordering of values has to lead to freedom." On this basis, he called for a classification of "values in a hierarchy such that freedom increasingly appears in it" (NFE, 9) so that the highest values would be those that are most closely connected to freedom. He went on to offer a first sketch of such a classification, in which he named as the highest values, in ascending order, passion, pleasure, criticism, and the demand for evidence, responsibility, creation, and, at the very top, generosity. (NFE, 470)

In assessing the contemporary relevance and significance of Sartre's ideas, it is important to recognize that he offered, though admittedly only in a somewhat embryonic form, a genuine alternative to all the positions that currently dominate the field of ethical theory, at least in the western world. For Sartre's theory would appear to be based on axiology, the study of values. And while it might seem obvious that an investigation into the nature and merits of the many kinds of values we encounter in the course of our experience could serve as the basis for a serious and promising approach to ethics, such an inquiry plays no significant role in any of the most prominent ethical theories on the recent or contemporary scene—including utilitarianism, deontological theories, virtue-based theories, social contract theories, religious theories based on an interpretation of God's commands or on some concept of "natural law," and sociological theories that conceive of ethical systems as socially constructed cultural projects that can achieve only a relative validity.

While Sartre was not the first ethicist to offer a hierarchical list of values, or to suggest that an understanding of the nature of these values—of their relations to one another, and of the ways in which they differ from one another in moral significance and importance—might serve as the centerpiece of a defensible ethical theory, what is distinctive in Sartre's axiology is the primacy he assigned to the value of freedom. To see the force of this, consider how his position differs from classical utilitarianism, which takes happiness to be the central value, indeed the only thing that is intrinsically valuable. The classical utilitarianism of the 19th-century British philosophers Jeremy Bentham and John Stuart Mill holds that all other positive values—health, intelligence, friendship, beauty, and so forth—are good only where they promote happiness and/or diminish unhappiness. Further, utilitarianism is a consequentialist ethical theory. It maintains that the rightness or wrongness of an action depends entirely upon the goodness or badness of its rationally foreseeable consequences. Thus, for a classical utilitarian, the right action in any circumstance is, in comparison to all other actions that might have been performed, the one that can be expected to produce the greatest amount of net happiness for the greatest number of individuals.

To see how Sartre's freedom-based axiological theory differs from utilitarianism, consider slavery. In assessing the rightness or wrongness of enslaving people, the utilitarian would inquire into the amount of happiness and unhappiness such a practice would bring to the various people who would be affected by it. To be fair to the utilitarians, we must concede that in almost all circumstances utilitarianism would condemn the practice of slavery as immoral. That's because slavery brings such misery to those who are enslaved that, even taking into account the happiness that others might derive from it (such as the happiness of the slave owners who would benefit from seeing their labor costs radically diminished, and that of consumers who might be offered the fruits of that inexpensive slave labor at a reduced price), it is difficult to think of circumstances in which enslaving people would produce a higher net balance of happiness over unhappiness than any other action that could be performed. Still, utilitarianism is open to the criticism that (a) it does not condemn slavery on principle, but rather does so only contingently, on the basis of a cost/benefit analysis; and (b) in carrying out that cost/benefit analysis, it has to count the happiness that slave owners derive from owning slaves as a good thing. Similarly, utilitarianism condemns my actions of coercing you or lying to you only if such actions fail to yield optimum results in terms of net happiness. And in calculating the effects of my lies and acts of coercion, the pleasure I get from doing these things is assigned the same moral significance as is the pain you experience as a result of them. And any other effects you might experience that do not result specifically in a lessening of your happiness, but might otherwise be presumed to be negative, are to be dismissed from consideration as morally irrelevant.

Sartre's theory, by contrast, produces a much quicker and more straightforward rejection of slavery. For while he readily acknowledged that pleasure is a positive value, it ranks rather low on his scale of values, and certainly cannot compete with freedom as a value. Thus, slavery, along with lesser kinds of coercion, cannot be justified on the basis of the pleasures they produce for those who enslave or coerce others since such practices subordinate a greater value to a lesser one.

Similarly, lying is to be condemned because it diminishes freedom. In order to carry out one's freely chosen projects, accurate information is essential. If my project is to bring about a state of affairs X, I need causal knowledge as to what sorts of actions can produce X. Ignorance of this, or worse, incorrect information about it, will probably cause my project to end in failure. Thus, lying, which amounts to the intentional transmission of incorrect information, has the effect of thwarting freely undertaken projects. So lying is morally indefensible when it is done for the purpose of producing pleasure and is justified only in those rare cases when it is necessary for the preservation or enhancement of freedom (as when one lies to a murderer about the whereabouts of his intended victim).

While coercion and deception stand as clear examples of disvalues in Sartre's axiology, since they diminish freedom, the positive value that stands at the summit of Sartre's value hierarchy is generosity, because it is the one in which freedom is most fully manifested. In an act of generosity one freely adopts another's end as one's own, and actively assists the other to achieve the realization of that end.

Generosity is founded on the idea that "what is wanted by one freedom must be accepted as such by other freedoms, simply because it is a freedom that wants it..." (NFE, 274-75)

To be sure, I should not help a person who is pursuing evil ends. But my default assumption is that the other's ends are not evil, and thus that it is good that these ends be realized, simply because they are freely sought by someone:

> One *first* has a tendency to help someone to pursue and realize his end, whatever it may be. This is a favorable prejudgment. *Afterwards*, but only afterwards, comes the idea that this end may be incompatible with my own ends or with a system of values to which I adhere. What we have is a *willingness to oblige*, whose extent is infinitely wider than we may believe and whose principle is: every end is good, as a future realization of value, until the contrary is demonstrated. If I ask a passerby to indicate a street to me, it may be in order to steal something or to commit a crime. Distrust would have the passerby assure himself that my goals are not bad ones. He does not do so. Not because he necessarily assumes that these goals are *moral*, but because *a priori* he posits that it is good that a goal be attained. (NFE, 275)

Sartre offered an example:

I am on the platform of the bus and I extend my hand to help the person running after the bus to get on board. In extending my hand I am a form of activity. In my very act of extending my hand my intention of helping is manifested....

I am a *gift*, that is, this hand that I am stretching out is there to be taken. At first glance and in its initial structure, it is there for him to grab like any pole or hand hold in the world. The act consisted in making a supplementary hand hold appear in the universe. So the result of this gift was my making myself a passivity in the world. What is more, I extend this hand toward him so that he will transform it into a body for others, so that he will take hold of it like a drowning man who clings to a branch, and so that he perceives it just like a branch. I freely make myself a passivity. The help here is a *passion*, an incarnation.

And, furthermore, in this gift of myself, I do not seek my own ends, rather I submit myself to his.... So I am exposing myself to a freedom that pierces me, that grasps me as an instrument of its own future....

Yet, reciprocally, the other does not grasp my hand as a fist. He has interpreted my gesture. He counts on my resistance to his weight, he is well aware that this hand is not put forth inadvertently and that I will not pull it back in surprise if he takes hold of it. Something new has appeared for him in his situation, an unexpected, undetermined *creation*, a first beginning that modifies this situation for him from top to bottom by leading him to make a new choice. And in and through this outstretched hand he suddenly *comprehends* another's end. The hand is outstretched so *that* he should take hold of it.... If he does do so, he is conscious of making an alien end exist, an end set before him by another freedom. He is conscious of helping this freedom to help him.... (NFE, 285-86)

In "What is Literature?" Sartre also described the interaction between writers and readers in terms of "generosity." Without readers, a writer's words fail to come to life. They simply lie there, abstract black shapes on white paper, completely dead and utterly devoid of meaning. "The creation can find its fulfillment only in reading,... [so] the artist must entrust to another the job of carrying out what he has begun.... Thus, the writer appeals to the reader's freedom to collaborate in the production of his work." (WIL, 54) Indeed, "reading is directed creation." (WIL, 53). Readers must freely make the decision to read, and then must exercise their freedom in interpreting and making sense of the writer's text. And in doing so, they recognize that what they are interpreting is not some portion of the natural world, but rather the fruit of the writer's creativity—that is, a product of freedom. "Thus, reading is an exercise in generosity.... The reader's feelings ... have their permanent source in freedom; that is, they are all generous—for I call a feeling generous which has its origin and its end in freedom." (WIL, 58)

And with freedom comes responsibility. Every literary creation, according to Sartre, must necessarily, even if unintentionally, and even if only implicitly, present a philosophy—a general view of what is true, and important, and good. This creates a responsibility on the part of writers to consider consciously whether their work, should it find readers, will help to promote a better world, or will it instead, even if only unwittingly, help to perpetuate oppression and injustice, and stand as an obstacle to moral and political progress. Though many writers may try to evade this responsibility by adopting a posture of neutrality, such a stance in fact has the effect, in a world in which structures are already in place, of lending support to the status quo. The writer's proper task is to "reveal," and thus to combat ignorance and claims of innocence—claims that can be used to justify passivity and the evasion of responsibility on the part of their readers. "To write is ... both to disclose the world and to offer it as a task to the generosity of the reader." (WIL, 65) Writers thus bear a heavy responsibility—to disclose reality accurately, to deal with topics of vital importance, and to do so in a way that is fully respectful of the reader's freedom to respond.

Writers, in turn, also ask a great deal of readers. When a reader decides to read, the result is

> a pact of generosity between the author and reader. Each one trusts the other; each one counts on the other, demands of the other as much as he demands of himself. For this confidence is itself generosity. Nothing can force the author to believe that his reader will use his freedom; nothing can force the reader to believe that the author has used his. Both of them make a free decision. There is then established a dialectical going-and-coming; when I read, I make demands; if my demands are met, what I am then reading provokes me to demand more of the author, which means to demand of the author that he demand more of me. And, vice versa, the author's demand is that I carry my demands to the highest pitch. Thus, my freedom, by revealing itself, reveals the freedom of the other (WIL, 61-62).

It is in the light of this point about the mutual demands of readers and writers that Sartre's naming "criticism and the demand for evidence" as a freedom-laden value is to be understood. Notice that when writers present a logical, evidence-based argument for some conclusion, they are making a noncoercive appeal to the freedom of their readers to assess the cogency of the argument, and then to decide, on that basis, whether to give voluntary assent to its conclusion. It is not as if the writer were asking his or her readers to accept the conclusion based on faith, authority, tradition, or fear of being punished for the heresy of disagreeing with it. And the readers, for the same reason, are right to demand evidence as a precondition for their willingness to give their assent to an author's conclusions. Rational criticism is likewise noncoercive and respectful of freedom. It is on the basis of the give-and-take of such criticism that we engage in a collaborative project of selectively rejecting, affirming, and revising our hypotheses so that our disclosures of reality might achieve progressively greater levels of accuracy.

3. Consciousness

Another aspect of Sartre's work that is especially important today is his description and analysis of consciousness. To be conscious is to be aware of things, to perceive, feel, imagine, or remember them, to have subjective experiences of various kinds, and thus to access the "qualia" of things—that is, the qualitative aspect involved in encountering them. Through conscious experiences, we learn "what it's like" to see the color red, to hear a sad song, to feel the warmth of the sun on the back of our neck, or the coldness of an ice cube pressed against our flesh, to remember how it felt to fall in love, to fantasize about winning a gold medal at the Olympics, to taste fresh strawberries, to smell the discharge of a skunk, and to experience victory and defeat, triumph and disappointment, energy and fatigue, health and sickness, pleasure and pain, and a million other things.

Why is Sartre's contribution to the understanding of consciousness important? One reason is that very little significant philosophical work has addressed this topic. Moreover, given that phenomenology is a comparatively recent development in philosophy (it is usually said to have begun in 1900, with the publication of Edmund Husserl's *Logical Investigations*), Sartre's work in this area might well be characterized as pioneering.

Why has the study of consciousness been neglected? The major reason seems to be that consciousness can neither be observed nor measured. By contrast, behavior is both observable and measurable, and in recent years the same has become true of brain activity. Thus, it has seemed to many that the study of behavior and/or of neural functioning could be "objective" in a way that the study of consciousness could not. It was then reasonable to make the case that studying behavior and the brain might make for a more promising research program than would studying consciousness. From there, it was easy to slide into the more dubious hypothesis that consciousness could simply be *reduced* to behavior and neural activity, and then for that to morph into the even more radical view that consciousness is an illusion and does not exist at all.

Within French thought, Sartre's great forerunner in the study of consciousness was René Descartes, the 17th-century philosopher, mathematician, and scientist who is often called "the father of modern philosophy." Perhaps Descartes' greatest philosophical achievement was his demonstration that consciousness is the unique and universal medium of access to whatever exists, that it is only by means of consciousness that we can be aware of anything at all.

But Descartes made certain mistakes, some of which unwittingly helped to facilitate the rise of consciousness-denial. One such mistake was to conceive of consciousness as a substance—that is, as a kind of thing. Another error was to insist that this substance was wholly spiritual in character. In contrast to physical things, which are extended in space, Descartes insisted that consciousness, also called "mind" or "spirit," did not exist in space at all. This claim gave rise to numerous insoluble difficulties. For example, Descartes upheld the common-sense notion that mind and body interact, as when a hard blow to the body gives rise to conscious experiences of pain, or when a mental decision to get out of a chair and walk to the kitchen results in the body taking precisely this action. But if the mind and body are capable of such causal interaction, one wonders *where* such interaction could possibly take place, and *how*, exactly, a nonphysical substance could produce effects in the physical world (and vice versa).

Descartes' separation of mind and body into two radically distinct kinds of substances gave rise to a research program within western philosophy in which consciousness was investigated as if it were a kind of thing, with the main focus of inquiry directed toward the task of figuring out how consciousness can causally interact with bodies. Little attention was paid to conscious experience itself, to its modes or structures, or to its objects conceived of as such (that is, considered in terms of their nature *as* objects of conscious experience, as opposed to their being understood in terms of their independent existence apart from our conscious awareness). The fruitlessness of Cartesian research led to a gradual loss of interest in the nature of consciousness, and a steadily increasing interest in philosophical naturalism—that is, the idea that everything arises from natural properties and causes, with supernatural or spiritual explanations specifically excluded or discounted. The Cartesian notion of a purely spiritual, nonphysical mind that could "inhabit," and direct or animate, an otherwise lifeless body, and that could detach itself from that body upon the body's death and go on to live without it, began increasingly to look like a primitive, unscientific superstition. As a result, by the 19th century, the investigation of consciousness and subjectivity had largely been banished as a respectable philosophical topic. The rise of behaviorism—roughly, the idea that everything organisms do can be best understood solely in terms of overt bodily movements that are observable and measurable, with no reference at all to conscious experiences—helped to kill it off, as did the subsequent introduction of technology allowing direct observation of brain activity. These developments have contributed to the widespread neglect of consciousness as a subject of research.

Phenomenology, in radical contrast, is devoted precisely to the study of conscious experiences of all kinds. It attempts to identify and describe the essential structures of experience. It studies the objects of experience as phenomena—that is, just as they appear to consciousness, and also investigates the various acts of consciousness, such as perceiving, thinking, imagining, remembering, questioning, doubting, loving, hating, and so forth, by and through which such phenomena are disclosed. Phenomenology attempts to avoid any assumptions about what is or is not real that are not rigorously grounded in the data of experience itself. Similarly, in its quest to describe the entire world as given in experience, it refuses to restrict its focus to those aspects of experience that are objective in some obvious and uncontroversial sense, and are easy to quantify. Accordingly, it takes an interest in all varieties of experience—not only sense experience, but also logical, mathematical, moral, political, and aesthetic experience. Many of the objects of our conscious experience are not in any straightforward way encountered by means of any of our five senses. One can think about the number 7, and fully grasp some principle of logic (such as that if either A is true or B is true, but A is not true, then B must be true), even though numbers and logical principles are inaccessible to the senses. Similarly, while one might observe, and be outraged by, an act of gross injustice, one does not technically "see" with any sense organ the injustice itself. Some conclude that injustice is therefore wholly subjective—something that we simply project onto the world. But phenomenology insists that such a conclusion not be asserted based on some metaphysical theory about what is and is not real, maintaining that it would be premature to use such theorizing to prejudge an investigation into what is disclosed in our experiences of injustice.

In Sartre's phenomenological writings on consciousness, he retained Descartes' views on the centrality of consciousness to all of our awareness and knowledge, as well as his refusal to limit our knowledge-producing experience to sense experience. Descartes is often classified as a "rationalist" because he argued that reason—that is, thinking, the use of logic in the analysis of concepts—is a more reliable and fundamental source of knowledge than sense experience.

But Sartre jettisoned almost every other aspect of Descartes' conception of consciousness. For starters, he categorically rejected the idea that consciousness is a substance—that is, a kind of thing or container of things. On the contrary, it is better conceptualized as an activity. Consciousness does not take things, or even representations of things, inside itself because, as an activity rather than a thing, it has no inside. It is a directedness toward objects, a revealing of them, a focusing on them, rather than a place that might serve as a repository for them.

Thus, to contrast "consciousness" and "body" as two different kinds of substances, as Descartes did, is to commit a kind of category mistake, akin to contrasting "body" with "running" or "breathing." For running and breathing are not different kinds of *things* than the body, but rather different *activities* that can be *performed* by a body. And included among the actions that are well within the ability of most human bodies are those that we associate with consciousness and the mind, most notably being aware of things—that is, sensing them, thinking about them, imagining them, remembering them, and so forth.

Embodiment

So Sartre also rejected Descartes' conception of consciousness or mind as pure spirit, separable and distinct from the body. In Sartre's view, the body is not an inert lump of matter that comes alive only when a spirit inhabits and animates it. Rather, the living body is itself conscious. Or, to put it another way, consciousness is embodied. Indeed, he insisted that consciousness is "wholly body," and that "the body is wholly 'psychic.'" (BN, 404) Consciousness is diffused throughout the body. My body is not something I "have" or "own." It is more accurate to say that I *am* my body. Though my body is undeniably a physical object (it has a definite size, shape, and spatial location, and is subject to gravity and other physical laws), it is nonetheless more accurate to say that it is *me*, rather than that it is an object of mine. As Sartre put it, my body is "an instrumental center of instrumental complexes..., *a point of view and a point of departure.*" (BN, 429-430)

To grasp Sartre's point, consider what is involved in riding a bicycle, changing a light bulb, typing a document, or, indeed, undertaking any physical action whatsoever. If the body were a mindless lump of matter that a mind had to direct, then my procedure in performing one of these actions would be to use my body parts as if they were tools. But that is not what happens. Rather, when doing one of these things, it is my body that acts; or, if you prefer, I act through my body. When playing catch in the backyard, I don't instruct or direct my hand to reach up for a high throw. Rather, I reach up for it—my hand is part of me, not an instrument I manipulate.

Or consider what is involved in using a tool: "I do not apprehend my hand in the act of writing but only the pen which is writing; this means that I use my pen in order to form letters but not my hand in order to hold the pen. I am not in relation to my hand in the same utilizing attitude as I am in relation to the pen; I *am* my hand.... The hand is only the utilization of the pen." (BN, 426)

Similarly, we typically experience the bodies of other people as incarnated consciousnesses. "The Other is originally given to me as a body in situation." We do not encounter it as merely one physical thing among others, "as if it were an isolated object having purely external relations with other [things]. That is true only for a corpse. The Other's body as flesh is immediately given as the center of reference in a situation which is synthetically organized around it." (BN, 451)

While some bodies are not conscious, for example, those that are dead, all consciousnesses are embodied. My body is "in no way a contingent addition to my soul; on the contrary it is a permanent structure of my being and the permanent condition of possibility for my consciousness as consciousness of the world and as a transcendent project toward my future." (BN, 431)

But while Sartre clearly rejected the Cartesian account, according to which consciousness is separable from the body, this does not mean that he adopted the widespread program of simply reducing conscious acts, together with the qualia disclosed by them, to the underlying physiological conditions that enable and sustain them. To reduce the content of an experience to the physical and physiological conditions that help to produce it is simply to conflate effect and cause. If there were no difference in principle between the qualitative content of the experiences of seeing different colors, it would not be possible to discover which physical conditions are correlated with experiences of which colors.

Intentionality

Consciousness, in its essence, is awareness. But to be aware is to be aware *of something*. So consciousness always takes an object. Consciousness is not a thing, but rather a *relation*—a directedness toward objects, an "aboutness" of them, a way of "having" them. In understanding consciousness this way, Sartre was a faithful follower of Edmund Husserl, the German philosopher who was the principal founder of phenomenology. Husserl famously, and repeatedly declared that "all consciousness is consciousness of something." To perceive is to perceive something; and there is no imagining without something imagined, nor remembering without something remembered, loving without something loved, judging without something judged, fearing without something feared, or fantasizing without something about which one fantasizes. Husserl's and Sartre's name for this essential feature of consciousness, its "taking" objects, or being "pointed" toward them, is "intentionality." Conscious acts aim at, are about, "intend" some object. It is only by means of intentionality that one can be "presented" with an object. Moreover, intentionality, this correlativity of the conscious act and its object, is a feature of *all* conscious experience. It is not as if consciousness were first something in and of itself, and then later had the capacity to enter into a relation with something else. Rather, consciousness is *essentially* relational, and oriented toward objects.

"Intentionality" thus names a relation that is utterly unique, totally different from any other kind of relation in the world. In particular, the relation uniting any conscious act (say, that of seeing) with its object (the thing seen) differs from any kind of causal relationship. To see a tree in my backyard, to notice that it is taller than the roof of my garage, and to grasp the logical point that it must therefore also be taller than anything else that is shorter than the roof of my garage, is not to *cause* the tree to exist, or to be located in my backyard, or to be taller or shorter than anything else. Nor is it to move the tree, or cut it in half, or alter its color or temperature, or enter into any other kind of causal relationship with it. The "intentional" acts of seeing, or thinking about, or imagining, or remembering something is not to interact causally with the thing seen, thought about, imagined, or remembered. The intentional act of "having" an object is an entirely different kind of relation to that object.

Another way of making this point is to say that the intentional relation between a conscious act and the object toward which it is directed is unlike any kind of purely physical relation. No purely physical interactions among physical objects are anything like the relationship between the act of judging and the thing judged, or between imagining and the thing imagined, seeing and the thing seen, recalling and the thing recalled, and so forth. For the connection between consciousness and the objects it intends is one of meanings, rational justifications, insight, understanding, and the like. Nonconscious objects are in no sense related to one another in this way. To explain a belief in terms of meanings, concepts, purposes, reasons, evidence, logical inferences, and argument is not to explain it in terms of any kind of physical laws or mechanistic causality, nor in terms of some other kind of causality (such as that of psychological laws) that might be thought to derive from them. Causal explanation and rational justification are utterly different from one another, and it is the latter that is facilitated by the unique kind of relation between consciousness and its objects that is called "intentionality."

Another important point that Husserl, Sartre, and other phenomenologists made about consciousness is that it is not passive, but active, as the term "intentionality" suggests. To be aware of anything, one must engage in active, selective focusing, and one must make choices. One must choose, first of all, among the many different kinds of conscious actions to undertake—that is, whether to look at something in one's visual field, or instead to think about some issue or problem, or to engage in an act of imagination, or of recollection. Then there are choices to be made toward the object on which one will be focusing—what to look at, think about, imagine, or remember. And there are also choices regarding the particular way in which one will focus on the object in question—which aspects of it will engage one's attention; in light of what question or project will one regard it; and under the heading of what concepts or categories? In looking at a physical object, for example, one might focus on its size, shape, color, texture, or features that would make it a useful tool for some task, or some way in which it resembles, or contrasts with, something else in the visual field, and so on endlessly. Thus, in looking at a tomato, one might see, based on the nature of one's selective focusing, a red thing, or a round thing, or a thing of a certain size, or an organic thing, or an edible thing, or an item that is on sale in the grocery store, and so forth. The tomato does not tell us how to look at it. Nor, for that matter, do the various items in my visual field conspire to tell me how to organize them in a perceptual act. Rather, everything depends on the nature and direction of my selective focusing.

In speaking of choices in this context, I don't mean to suggest that one must separately choose *whether* to look, *what* to look at, *how* to look, and so forth. Instead, one decision typically entails most or all of the others. In most cases, a person quite spontaneously notices things that are strongly relevant to the project in which he or she is engaged, and in so doing, focuses on the specific aspects of those things that are most relevant to the project. So while it is in a sense misleading to speak in terms of "choice" when referring to the act of focusing on an item in one's visual field, since one does not usually make an explicit decision to focus in this way, it is nonetheless true that such acts usually result directly from the undertaking of projects that are consciously chosen. One who has decided to examine a crime scene for clues leading to the identity of the perpetrator does not have to make an additional decision as to whether or not to look for fingerprints, hair, blood, fibers, footprints, and the like.

In discussing the selective activity of consciousness, Sartre often made use of the notion, derived from Gestalt psychology, of the distinction between figure and ground. The basic idea is that in all conscious acts, there is something on which attention is focused, and other things that might have been clearly noticed—but which, precisely because they are not attended to—fade into the background and are noticed only vaguely, if at all. We perceive a figure on the ground, and the activity of our consciousness in doing so is indicated by the fact that the world does not organize itself in this way for us.

Sartre claimed that such an organization of the perceptual field is typically achieved instantly, at the very moment that a given perceptual act commences, especially when the perceiver is engaged in a project, and thus looking at the world while in pursuit of some end. Here, Sartre's view opposed some classical empiricists who claim that in perception we first encounter raw sense data, which we only subsequently assemble into objects. Such a claim is phenomenologically inaccurate. It fails as a description of what our experience is like. We do not typically begin by noticing specific shapes, colors, textures, smells, sounds, and so forth, which we then synthesize and analyze, before ultimately arriving at an awareness of objects. Rather, we aim at objects directly through intentional acts, and it is usually these that we encounter right from the outset, noticing discrete bits of sense data only on those relatively rare occasions when we deliberately focus on them—an act of abstraction that requires us to shift our attention away from the objects with which we are typically engaged. From a phenomenological standpoint, we live in a world of objects, rather than a world of bits of color and sound.

A similar point could be made in connection with the observation, much emphasized by Husserl and fully endorsed by Sartre, that we can never see all sides of a physical object at once, but rather must always see it only in profile. When we look at the front of a house, we cannot see the back, and vice versa. If we go up in the air to observe its top, the roof, from above, we cannot simultaneously see the bottom of the house, from below. All visual perception is partial and perspectival in this sense. Still, despite the incompleteness of the image that strikes our optic nerve, it is not accurate to say that I first see a "house part," or façade, and then, drawing on my background knowledge about houses, make the inference that there are other sides that I am not seeing, and that the object in front of me is a house. Instead, I "see," right from the beginning, much more than merely what strikes my optic nerve. I see a house from the front, rather than the front of a house.

Thus, the coherent and unified experience of objects in the world requires considerable conscious activity. Not only must I be able to "look past" the profiles of things, and the raw sense data underlying my perception of them, in order to "see" an object, but I must also be able to synthesize different perceptual experiences and fuse them with memory and with imagination. I have to be able to perceive that the house I am now seeing from the back is the same as the one I just saw from the front, and the same as the one I remember seeing two weeks ago, and the same as the one I anticipate seeing again tomorrow. Moreover, I must be aware of a great many ways in which the object perceived relates to other objects, if my experienced world is to make any sense at all. Consciousness is ceaselessly active and interpretive from the beginning. It does not passively receive and record sense impressions, but rather actively shapes, unifies, and synthesizes information in a way that enables a person to perceive unified objects and a coherent world. This requires a synthesis of perception, expectation, memory, and imagination. To understand what I am seeing right now, I must be able to grasp how it is related to what I was seeing just a moment ago, and how it pertains to what is likely to happen next (for example, think of what is involved in following the plot of a movie or play, or in hearing a sequence of notes as a melody).

Meaning

Thus, it is clear that it is only through intentionality, the activity of consciousness in aiming at objects, and selectively focusing on their various aspects, that meaning can emerge. To see something as meaningful is to see it *as* something. But to do that, one must focus on it in a selective way, so that some of its features are highlighted, while others recede into the background. To see something *as* something is to see *what* it is, at least partially or in some specific context. It is to see it under the heading of one set of concepts or categories at the expense of others. Which aspects of the thing are noticed usually depends on the interests of the observer, and the projects in which he or she is engaged. The meanings of things emerge when we ask *what* they are, what they are *for*, how they relate to other things, and so forth. If it were possible somehow to view the world without bringing a portion of it to the foreground through an act of selective focusing, motivated by the (at least implicit) asking of such questions, what would emerge would not be meaning, but only the bare, featureless fact of existence. And if it were possible to view the world without relegating to the background, other portions of it (those that are irrelevant to my present projects and fail to attract my interest on other grounds) through this same act of selective focusing, so that all the aspects of everything were simultaneously presented to my consciousness, the result would not be the emergence of meaning, but rather the drowning out of meaning in a cacophony of infinite, incoherent, and incommensurable meanings.

One way of grasping this point is to think about the difference between meaning, that is, the "whatness" of things, and existence, their sheer "is-ness" or "thatness." This is a major theme of Sartre's first novel, *Nausea*. Its protagonist, Antoine Roquentin, gradually develops a strange disability. He finds it increasingly difficult to see anything as something particular, that is, to notice some finite set of its attributes while ignoring others, and thus to encounter it under one set of concepts or categories at the expense of others. Words begin to seem to him inadequate as tools to use for referring to things. For things have a kind of infinite abundance that no finite set of words can capture. There is always more to them than we can notice at once, more to them than what is relevant to our current interests and projects, and more to them than we can ever think of or describe.

In his diary, Roquentin recounts his somewhat pathological encounter with a tram seat on which he had been sitting:

> I murmur: 'It's a seat,' rather like an exorcism. But the word remains on my lips, it refuses to go and put itself on the thing. It stays what it is, with its red plush, thousands of little red paws in the air, all stiff, little dead paws. This huge belly turned upwards, bleeding, puffed up–bloated with all its dead paws, this belly floating in this box, in this grey sky, is not a seat. It could just as well be a dead donkey, for example, swollen by the water and drifting along.... Things have broken free from their names. They are there, grotesque, stubborn, gigantic, and it seems ridiculous to call them seats or say anything at all about them.... (N, 180)

One cannot see a tram seat *as* a seat without focusing on it in a certain way, highlighting some of its features, excluding others from one's attention, and applying the relevant concepts to it. A different focus might produce a different experienced meaning, as one might then encounter a "red thing," or a "coarsely textured thing," or a "manufactured thing," rather than a seat. Moreover, in order fully to grasp that it is a "seat," one must understand something about the connection between it and a host of other objects, each of which must also be competently grasped and conceptualized. One must understand, for example, that people require rapid transportation from one place to another, that they wish to be comfortable and retain their energy while traveling, that sitting is often both more comfortable and less tiring than standing, and that the object in question has been specifically designed to facilitate seating, and has been placed in the tram for that purpose.

Were it possible to see the tram seat without these activities of consciousness, that is, without any specific conceptualization and not in connection with its relation to anything else, one would simply be seeing undifferentiated existence itself, that is, existence devoid of meaning. Meaning arises through the confrontation of an active, intending, focusing consciousness with the things of this world. It is a product of the relation between consciousness and its objects—yet another way in which that relation is unique, and utterly unlike the causal relations inherent in the interactions among nonconscious entities.

The fact that we encounter meanings routinely in our everyday lives illustrates another important phenomenological point: that it is possible to experience directly at least some things that are not accessible to the senses. For while we typically do have to take in some information through the senses in order to experience meaning, meaning itself is not something that is accessed via the senses in any direct or straightforward way.

Consider what is involved in the experience of understanding the meaning of spoken words immediately upon hearing them. While one must indeed undergo the sensory experience of hearing the sounds produced by the speaker in order to understand his or her meaning, it appears that one does not first attend to those sounds before deriving meaning from them through a process of inference and interpretation. Rather, one in some sense "looks past" the sensory content of the sounds in order to focus, right from the outset, on a non-sensory aspect of them—their meaning.

As evidence, notice that all the sensory aspects of the sounds produced by the speaker—their pitch and volume level, the timbral quality of the speaker's voice, the accent, and so forth—are irrelevant to the speaker's meaning, and listeners who are primarily interested in ascertaining that meaning pay little or no attention to them. Even the differences in the sounds of words such as "big" and "pig" are intrinsically irrelevant and attract little interest or attention. Their function is merely that of directing the hearer's attention to the difference in meaning, which could be marked by any convention. This point is rendered obvious by the fact that the same meaning could be conveyed in another spoken language with entirely different phonetic content, or by written words that produce no sound at all. No particular sensory content is necessary for conveying meaning, which is itself not sensory.

Consider this point in the light of Sartre's claim that in perception there is always the construction of a figure on a ground. When listening carefully to a speaker, one pushes into the background all sounds other than those produced by the speaker. One ignores, and scarcely notices, the sounds of people coughing, or blowing their noses, or fidgeting in their seats. Similarly, as noted, to the extent that one's primary interest is in the information or message that the speaker is communicating, one either pays only marginal attention to, or ignores entirely, the purely auditory aspects of the sounds that the speaker makes (that is, the high or a low pitch of the speaker's voice, its clear or gravelly timbre, its regular or irregular cadence, and so forth). One might assume, then, that what is being elevated to the foreground are those aspects of the speaker's sounds that are relevant to their being understood as words that convey meaning. But that is not phenomenologically accurate. Once again, one's focus is not on anything sensory at all, but rather on the meaning itself. As evidence for this, notice that a competent, attentive listener can often accurately convey the gist of a just-heard speech without being able to recall any of the specific words or phrases that the speaker had used.

Similarly, it would be a somewhat superficial analysis to say that when reading, one relegates the white paper to the background so as to focus on the black shapes that form letters, which in turn, form words, sentences, paragraphs, and so forth. Rather, it is descriptively more accurate to say that we also look past the black shapes, pushing them into a relatively undifferentiated background. Reading would be a laborious and unreasonably time-consuming activity if one first had to attend to the shape of black marks, then interpret them as constituting words, and then interpret a succession of words as constituting a statement. Instead, a skilled and experienced reader recognizes words, and sometimes whole phrases, as one recognizes a familiar face. One doesn't recognize a face by first noticing a certain shape of the chin, then of the nose, then of the forehead, and then of the mouth, in order finally, through a process of synthesis and analysis, to draw the inference that this must be Bill. To be sure, were any of these features substantially altered, we would not recognize the face as Bill's. But if they have not been altered, we identify Bill's face in a flash, as a gestalt, that is as an organized whole, perceived as such, not based on a summary analysis of its parts. We see Bill's face typically without focusing on or noticing the shape of his nose, or any other specific facial feature. Similarly, when reading, we "look past" and pay little or no attention to the shapes of letters, the letters themselves, and even the words and phrases that are constructed from those letters. Our focus, instead, is on something non-sensory: the meanings that the words and phrases convey. And it is these that we typically recall, even if we retain no recollection at all of the author's specific words.

What is true of meanings appears also to be true of values: they are objects of direct experience, even though they are inaccessible to the senses. To see an older, bigger child beat a younger, smaller one, without provocation, is to see, in addition to the relevant observable physical events (such as a fist impacting a face), cruelty, injustice, and wrongness—in spite of the fact that none of these things are straightforwardly available to the senses. Injustice has no shape or color, and yet we somehow "see" it.

Ego

Sartre's claim that consciousness is an activity, rather than a substance, and that it attentively *goes out toward* objects in the world, as opposed to taking representations of those objects *inside itself*, goes against the "common sense" view of consciousness, as well as the conception defended by many philosophers. Even more radical was his rejection of the idea that there is a "transcendental ego" standing behind, initiating, and directing all conscious acts. According to many philosophers, most notably Immanuel Kant, but also Sartre's hero, Edmund Husserl (in his later works), it is the activity of this ego (or "I" or "self") that accounts for the unity of my conscious acts. It is what makes all of my experiences uniquely "mine," and explains why they form a coherent stream, rather than a random, jumbled, unconnected collection.

Sartre's case against the transcendental ego rests primarily on two central claims—that we never encounter such an ego in our experience, and that we do not need to postulate its existence in order to explain what we do find in experience. He also offered an explanation as to why we tend to fall into the error of believing in a transcendental ego. This is relevant to his case insofar as it serves as a response to those who would take the widespread belief in such an ego as evidence of its existence.

In maintaining that we do not encounter the presence of an "I" underlying our conscious experiences, Sartre placed himself, once again, in opposition to Descartes, who had argued that precisely such a presence was given to us in reflective experience with a degree of clarity and distinctness that could not be matched by any other experiential datum. Indeed, the most famous feature of Descartes' philosophy is his "I think, therefore I am" argument, which concludes that there is only one absolutely indubitable truth, one assertion that is so secure as to be worthy of serving as the foundation and starting point for all other knowledge—that an "I," as a thinking substance, exists wherever and whenever there is a thought.

Descartes' mistake, according to Sartre, was to overlook the significance of the fact that the "I" appears only in reflection, which is a secondary mode of consciousness. In every case in which it appears, it does so only after an episode of conscious activity of the primary sort, which Sartre called "consciousness in the first degree." (TE, 41) For consciousness in this "unreflected" or "pre-reflective" mode does not focus on itself, but rather directs itself "outward" toward objects in the world. For example, if I am counting, the content of my thought—what I am focusing on and thinking about—is not anything about myself, but rather "17, 18, 19, 20, 21," and so forth. It is only when my consciousness shifts to the reflective mode, taking its own activities for its objects, that the "I" is manifested, as in thoughts such as "I've been thinking about numbers all afternoon."

Consciousness | 53

This observation suggests the possibility that the "I" is not *discovered* in reflection, but rather is *constituted* in reflective acts of consciousness.

In any case, contrary to Descartes' famous claim, we never experience an "I" as a subject or substance directing our conscious acts. Most of the time, that is, while we are in the pre-reflective mode, we do not experience an "I" at all. But when we switch to the reflective mode, in which we focus on previously undertaken acts of pre-reflective consciousness, the "I" appears only as an object, never as a subject. We never observe it "in the act" of directing our conscious acts. The reflective consciousness that says, "I've been thinking about numbers," is distinct from the pre-reflective consciousness that actually was thinking about numbers. As Sartre put it, in responding to Descartes, "the consciousness which says *I Think* is precisely not the consciousness which thinks." (TE, 45)

But the fact that we do not encounter in experience an ego inhabiting or underlying consciousness does not prove that there is not one, or even that we cannot know that there is one. "Transcendental" means "relating to a spiritual or nonphysical realm," so perhaps it is unsurprising that something called a "transcendental ego" might not be the kind of thing one could encounter by means of ordinary experience. And Kant, in particular, is famous for introducing into philosophy the idea of a "transcendental" argument, by which he meant an inference, based on the fact that we experience and know certain things, that whatever is a necessary condition of our ability to experience and know what we do must also exist, even if it is inaccessible to our experience, and not knowable in any more direct fashion. Kant offered such an argument in support of the transcendental ego, maintaining that knowledge would not be possible without a self or "I" underlying our perceiving and thinking, synthesizing distinct sensations and subsuming them under certain concepts or categories of understanding. Since we have no direct access to this "I," and have no other way of acquiring information about it, we know nothing else about it other than that it must exist as a necessary condition of the knowledge that we do have.

How, then, did Sartre attempt to refute the argument that a transcendental ego, while not directly experienced, can be inferred to exist as a necessary condition for the possibility of experiencing what we do experience? He did so by arguing that he can adequately account, with his simpler, non-egological conception of consciousness, for everything that Kant and Husserl invoked the transcendental ego to explain.

Perhaps the first problem to consider is this. How it is that consciousness can be aware of what it is doing when it is in the pre-reflective mode? For example, if there is no "I" directing my consciousness when it is engaged in the activity of counting, and no "I" is included among the objects toward which that consciousness is directed, how does it nonetheless happen that when someone suddenly enters the room and interrupts my intense pre-reflective engagement with "22, 23, 24, and 25" to ask me what I am doing, I am able, instantly and effortlessly, to answer, "I am counting"?

In answering this question, Sartre drew another distinction. He distinguished the kind of awareness that is achieved when a consciousness focuses on an object directly, explicitly noticing it as a particular kind of thing, from the less distinct, more implicit kind of awareness that one attains in connection with items on which one does not directly focus or make the object of one's attention. The former kind of consciousness, as exemplified by the kind of awareness one has of a glass of water that one is looking at, and thinking of as "a glass of water," Sartre called "thetic" or "positional." But he also maintained, on phenomenological grounds, that one is always aware of much more than that on which one directly focuses. This kind of unfocused, implicit, horizonal awareness—for example, that the glass of water is sitting on a table, that it is not the table on which it sits, and that it is also distinct from my consciousness of it—Sartre called "nonthetic" or "non-positional." While the content of the nonthetic awareness accompanying any given instance of thetic awareness will, for the most part, vary from case to case, one thing, according to Sartre, is constant. Any pre-reflective thetic consciousness of anything is always accompanied by a nonthetic awareness of its own activities. Consciousness is always self-*aware*, even though it is only intermittently self-*reflective*. So there is no need to postulate any additional entity, let alone one that is inaccessible to experience, such as a transcendental ego, to explain how a consciousness can be aware of its own activities, since such self-awareness is something that consciousness is able to achieve on its own. And it is this self-awareness that explains why it is so easy to transition from the pre-reflective mode, in which I am not thinking about what I am doing (because I am, instead, simply doing it, and in so doing focusing on the relevant external objects—"22, 23, 24, 25," and so forth), to the reflective mode, in which I am able, instantly and effortlessly, to report accurately on what I've just been doing ("I am counting").

The idea that consciousness is always nonthetically self-aware also helps to explain the existence of what Sartre called "the empirical ego," that is, the ego-as-object, which we find in experience, as contrasted with the unexperienced transcendental ego, which Sartre rejected as nonexistent. Nonthetic self-awareness facilitates reflection, and when consciousness switches to the reflective mode, it focuses on and objectifies that self-awareness. The empirical ego, which is to say one's sense of his or her "self," is then constructed out of a synthesis of an indefinite (and constantly increasing) number of these objectifications. By noticing regularities and consistencies in its own history of actions and attitudes, a particular embodied consciousness develops an increasingly rich sense of its own distinctive characteristics. It begins to attribute to itself dispositions, tendencies, tastes, interests, and the like—in short, it comes to see itself as having a specific nature. Thus, by selectively recalling elements of its own past, and by synthesizing them—again, selectively—with its present attitudes and plans, and with its projected future actions, consciousness constructs an ego or sense of self.

While an empirical ego is built on the basis of observed regularities and consistencies in the history of a particular embodied consciousness, once it is constructed, the result is usually an increase in such consistency. For if I have a sense of self, that is, if I think of myself as being this rather than that kind of person, with a particular set of interests and concerns, and committed to these projects, values, goals, and ideals at the expense of others, this sense of self has some effect in terms of regulating and guiding my future choices and actions. In constructing an ego, I construct a value-system and a self-image, and these typically lead to a degree of inertia, as I choose to conform to this self-image. In Sartre's view, there is often an element of self-deception in this. I may think, "I can't do that, I'm not that kind of person," when in fact I remain free to act in ways that are different from the pattern I have established in the past, and at odds with my current self-image.

We are now in a position to take up the question that has given rise to the hypothesis that there must be a transcendental ego inhabiting or standing behind consciousness. To the extent that my many and various conscious experiences all seem to be uniquely mine, to go together to form a unified whole, and to make sense as such, rather than appearing as a haphazard, disconnected jumble, how can this be explained, given that I have no awareness of doing anything to achieve these effects myself? With his explanation of the nature and role of the empirical ego in place, Sartre contended that he could offer an alternative account of the unity, individuation, and coherence of my conscious experience—all the phenomena that the transcendental ego is traditionally invoked to explain. Moreover, he could claim superiority for his account, since, while it concedes nothing to its rival in terms of explanatory power, it is a simpler and less speculative theory because it does not have to postulate the existence of entities that are inaccessible to experience.

Sartre's alternative explanation appeals to a confluence of several factors. One, as just mentioned, is that consciousness selectively reflects on its prior activity, constructs out of this material a sense of self or ego, and then chooses to regulate its subsequent conduct (to some degree) by reference to this self-concept, thus introducing a degree of consistency and stability in that conduct that might otherwise have been absent.

Secondly, in *Being and Nothingness* Sartre pointed out that our conscious actions typically relate to one another instrumentally within a hierarchy of projects, according to the logic of means and ends. For example, I buy gasoline and put it in the car because I want to go to the grocery store to purchase food. I need to eat this food, so that I will have enough energy to get through my work this afternoon, which I want to do so I can maintain my job and avoid being fired, which I want to do so I can afford to continue to pay my rent, which I want because I don't want to be homeless and live on the street. These interconnections give to my actions a measure of internal coherence that they might otherwise have lacked.

A third factor is the fact that every consciousness is embodied, and essentially tied to one body. Thus, consciousnesses are already individuated, and require no external cause to bring about their individuation. By nature, your body differs somewhat from mine, so that our experiences will diverge slightly, even if we are doing more or less the same thing and focusing on the same objects in the same way and at the same time. Perhaps one of us is color-blind or has a more acute sense of smell, or greater upper body strength, than the other one. Further, the unity, durability, and continuity of each of our bodies contribute to the unity, durability, and continuity of our respective experiences. In this regard, conscious acts and experiences resemble many other kinds of objects and processes, in that they have their own lawlike ways of coming together and uniting without requiring an external organizing principle, such as a transcendental ego, to bring this about. There is nothing mysterious about this. And because our embodiment prevents us from ever being in exactly the same place at the same time, it guarantees that our respective experiential histories will differ from one another. Your experiences in Madagascar will be different from mine in Chicago, just as (though less dramatically) your experiences will be different if you are located next door, or in the room next to mine, or two feet to my left. Once again, it is not surprising that I am able, rather effortlessly, to distinguish my experience from yours, or that you are able to do the same.

Finally, Sartre argued at length in *Being and Nothingness*, in the famous section on "The Look," that my interactions with others contribute strongly to my sense of self as a stable entity. Suppose that while I am pre-reflectively engaged in some project, and thus firing my attention outward rather than thinking reflectively about myself, I suddenly notice that someone is looking at me, objectifying me, categorizing and judging me. Prior to my becoming aware of the Other's look, I had not been thinking about the nature of my action, or what my doing it implied about my character. My focus had been on what was "to be done," and on the precise means of doing it. It was only when my eyes happened to meet those of the Other, and I recognized in those eyes the expression of disapproval, that I suddenly realized that what I was doing was, for example, cowardly. In this way other people "freeze" me, assigning to me a fixed essence—that I am "a coward." While people differ one from another in the degree to which their sense of self is attained in this way, it is clear that for most people the perceived judgment of others is a major factor. I recognize that the Other's judgment of me is often more objective than my own judgment of myself, both because the Other's appraisal is more disinterested and unbiased, and because only the Other has access to my objectivity in the primary mode of consciousness, the pre-reflective. Thus, for most of us, the look of the Other is a major source of our sense of self. It is the judgment of the Other, rather than the existence of a transcendental ego underlying my different conscious acts, that gives me my sense of a relatively stable and coherent "me."

Sartre further clarified the nature of this "me" (that is, this empirical ego or empirical "self") by comparing it to a melody. A melody is not independent of the individual notes that comprise it, a distinct entity that somehow stands behind those notes, supporting and directing them. Instead, a melody is nothing other than a sequence of individual notes grasped in terms of their relations with one another and heard as a unity. Similarly, Sartre maintained that the empirical ego, or self, is not a pre-existent substance that directs and unifies a sequence of thoughts, feelings, and actions; rather, the self just *is* this sequence comprehended as a unity.

He completed his critique of the thesis that there is a transcendental ego underlying, directing, and unifying the actions of each consciousness by asking why the belief in this thesis is so widespread, given that we never experience such an ego, and that there is no need to postulate its existence in order to explain what we do find in experience. In answering this question, he advanced the hypothesis that the belief in a transcendental ego provides comfort, in that it shields us from an awareness of the degree of our freedom and responsibility. I need not worry that I will do dangerous or despicable things if I am convinced that my actions are directed by a stable "self," with a fixed, essential nature that would preclude me from ever undertaking such actions. But matters are quite different if my ego, far from being a subject and a force that determines what I will think, feel, and do, is instead merely an object, based on a summary of what I have thought, felt, and done. While I would like to think that my ego makes me, and in so doing constrains me from doing anything stupid or evil, the truth is that I make my ego, and I am only as constrained by it as I choose to be. As Sartre put it,

> Perhaps, in reality, the essential function of the ego is not so much theoretical as practical.... Perhaps the essential role of the ego is to mask from consciousness its very spontaneity.... Everything happens ... as if consciousness constituted the ego as a false representation of itself, as if consciousness hypnotized itself before this ego which it has constituted, absorbing itself in the ego as if to make the ego its guardian and its law.... (TE, 100-101)

While it may be true that most of my actions are predictable since they fit in well with my established "character" (or "self" or ego), Sartre attributed this to such factors as (a) the inertia of my ongoing projects, which are also typically interconnected in such a way that I can change one of them only by changing several others, (b) the fact that my consciousness mostly operates in the pre-reflective mode, where it is shielded from the critical resources of reflection, and (c) that I may simply choose not to act in a way that conflicts with my (perhaps flattering) self-image. But there is little comfort in that. If I merely choose to do what is good, safe, and wise now, I could also choose to do what is evil, dangerous, and stupid tomorrow. Hence, the attraction of the idea of a transcendental ego—better to think that my ego constrains me, preventing me from changing in undesirable ways, than to think that I remain always free to change my ego, simply by choosing to act in a manner that is inconsistent with it.

Imagination

One of Sartre's most important and enduring contributions to the study of conscious experience was his work on the imagination, a topic that engaged him throughout his career. His approach was phenomenological—he attempted to describe what is disclosed in experience about the nature both of imaginative experience and of the objects with which it deals, that is, imagined objects, or "imaginaries."

Sartre's main strategy in identifying and describing the nature of imaginaries was to point out some of the ways in which they differ from objects of sense perception. He found that perceptual objects exhibit an inexhaustible richness that imaginaries lack. Objects that are accessible to the senses never present themselves all at once, but rather always only in profile. There is always more, indeed infinitely more, to be observed in them than can be noticed from any one vantage point, in one act of focused looking—or listening, or touching, and so forth—and with one set of concepts, categories, purposes, and/or issues in mind. It is not just that in looking at the front of a thing we are not seeing its back, which remains to be discovered in a separate act of focusing from a different point of view, but also that perceptual objects contain an indefinite number of aspects or elements, enter into an indefinite number of relations with other objects, and are capable of providing answers to an indefinite number of questions that might be asked about them. By asking the right questions, conducting the right kind of investigations, and focusing on things in the right way, we can learn about their size, shape, and color; their origins, and the changes they have undergone over time; their chemical composition; the uses (if any) to which they have been put; what happens to them when they are cut in two or submerged in water; what we can see when we examine their surfaces under a microscope, and so on infinitely.

Imaginaries, in quite radical contrast, are not "massive" and inexhaustible in this way. They give themselves all at once, and are just as we imagine them. There are no hidden truths about them waiting to be discovered, because there is nothing more to them than what we imagine them to be. Suppose that I have just imagined an incident in which I was frantically running down a street and up a flight of stairs, in an attempt to escape an attack from an assailant. Suppose further that the point of interest in this fantasy was the threat of danger and the flight from that threat, so that in this scenario, as I imagined it, I paid no attention to the scenery, or to anything else that was not relevant to its central feature. In that case, were I subsequently to be asked whether the sky was cloudy when the assailant was chasing me, or what color jacket he was wearing, or how many steps were on the set of stairs I climbed during the chase, it would be impossible to answer. If the cloudiness of the sky, the color of the jacket, and the number of stairs were not part of the content given in my original act of imagining this scene, I cannot now go back to "look" again at the jacket or the stairs to determine their color or number. Assigning a color and number now would be a case of altering the original imagined scene by adding some elements to it, as opposed to one of discovering already existing properties of the imagined objects. Imaginary objects, in short, contain only what we put into them as we mentally visualize them.

On the other hand, had I been chased by a real assailant, it would have been possible, afterward, to go back and count the number of stairs I had climbed (even though, just as in the case of the imagined scene, I likely wouldn't have noted their number as I was climbing them). Similarly, it might well have been possible to determine, after the fact, the cloudiness of the sky (meteorologists keep a record of such things), and the color of the assailant's jacket (perhaps he was captured and arrested while wearing it, or photographed while chasing me, or observed by multiple witnesses who noted such details in order to be able to provide a complete and accurate description to the police). In short, objects that are perceived through the senses, rather than imagined, contain more, indeed infinitely more, than we find in any one perceptual encounter with them, or in any finite number of such encounters.

This helps to explain the fact that we typically experience objects of sense perception as "real" and "present" to consciousness, while imaginaries appear to be "unreal," either in the sense of being utterly nonexistent or at least as not here now. The rich, endless, detail with which perceived objects present themselves is experienced as something *discovered*, not as something that we had created and that we could change effortlessly through an act of consciousness—and all of this is in direct contrast with our experience of imaginaries. Perceptual objects give themselves in experience with qualities that are strongly suggestive of real, independent existence, such as stubbornness, obtrusiveness, and a capacity to resist us in the carrying out of our projects—qualities that for the most part are lacking in our encounters with imaginaries.

These findings are consistent with those achieved when we shift our focus away from the objects of experience and toward the conscious acts that disclose them. For when we attend reflectively to the nature of our experience of imagining things, we find that it differs from perceptual experience just as much as imaginaries differ from perceptual objects. Although there is a creative aspect to perception, since our particular way of focusing on an object, and thus elevating some portion or aspect of it to the foreground while relegating other portions or aspects to the background, is up to us; the nature of the object, once our focus is fixed, largely determines the content of our perceptual experience. In this sense, perceiving, in contrast to imagining, is experienced as responsive rather than purely creative. In perception, we have the sense, which is an essential component of the experience, that we are encountering something independent of us, something that constrains our perceptive response within rather strict limits. In this way, it differs sharply from imaginative experience, which presents itself as spontaneous, creative, and free, and as confronting no constraints other than those it freely imposes on itself.

4. Freedom

As a philosopher, Sartre is known, above all else, as a defender of freedom, and as an opponent of determinism. The main determinist argument is simply that all events are ruled by the principle of causality, and that this must also therefore be true of human actions, since these are events. In challenging this argument, Sartre did not dispute the premise that all events are caused. Instead, he attempted to show that actions are not mere "events."

According to determinism, the future is not really open, but rather is fixed now. What happens next will result from what is going on now, just as the events occurring now are doing so because of what transpired in the past. This thesis of determinism by universal, unbroken causation is not to be confused with fatalism, or the doctrine of "predestination"—the radically unscientific view that everything must unfold in a certain way in order to conform to some pre-established "plan" that we are powerless to alter. On the contrary, determinism, if anything, is a hyper-scientific doctrine under which everything takes place strictly in accordance with physical laws. According to this view, there is a causal explanation for everything that happens, such that nothing other than what did in fact happen could have happened, given the antecedent conditions and the application of the relevant physical laws. Similarly, in this view, all the "choices" that you make are in fact necessitated in this same way and could not have been other than what they in fact turned out to be. Even if the choice seems very much to flow from you, rather than from any external causal source—you did exactly what you wanted to do, because of your desires, concerns, principles, and character—a determinist will still insist that these seemingly subjective and personal factors are themselves the necessary effects of prior causes. You have the character you have, with its characteristic desires and priorities, precisely because of a complex causal nexus that includes your genetic inheritance and all of your life experiences up to now—with each of these factors, in turn, having come about as a necessary result of past causes.

Note that when we are dealing with purely physical matters, we always assume that there is a causal explanation as to why things happen the way they do. If the car won't start, we do not accept as an "explanation" that it was a random, uncaused event, a break with all prior chains of causality, the absolutely novel first step in a new chain, a bold venture into an open, undetermined future. Rather, we investigate and we find, for example, that the lights were left on all night, draining the battery. Once we discover this, we not only know why the car didn't start, but also that it couldn't possibly have started. The dead battery was a causal antecedent that brought about not a mere possibility, but a necessity—it couldn't have been otherwise.

Why should we assume anything different about human actions? They, too, appear not to be random, but rather to be easily explainable, and even predictable, in the light of our knowledge of the actor's projects, interests, desires, and character. Each of these factors is also explainable as having come about as a result of prior causes. To say that such factors as these do not always require the undertaking of a specific action, but rather leave the actor "free" to choose from some indeterminate number of possible, mutually incompatible, actions, is to say that there is a break in the causal order, that what has happened up to now does not determine what happens next, that the history of causes flowing from the distant past up through the present still leaves the future open, that history is compatible with an indefinite number of possible futures. The determinist argument, then, is that the affirmation of freedom of choice in this sense commits us either to an inconsistency (if we still claim that everything that happens does so out of necessity in accordance with the law of cause and effect) or to the granting of an irrational and unjustified exception to an otherwise universal principle (if we claim that human actions are the one kind of event that evades the otherwise universal principle of causation). Or, if that is overstating it, the determinist would at least argue that the doctrine of freedom of choice violates the principle of parsimony, because it requires us to adopt a messy, complicated theory as to how things happen (sometimes by means of causal necessitation, and sometimes by means of free choice), over the neat, clean, straightforward doctrine that everything happens in the same way—because it was made to do so by prior causes.

But the partisans of freedom can reply that just as it is powerfully evident to us in many contexts that everything happens in accordance with the law of cause and effect—so that we would reject as absurd the hypothesis that the car's failure to start was uncaused—so is it equally evident to us that, when making a choice, we have available to us alternate futures, as the history of the universe and the laws of physics do not leave us with only one option. To take a rather trivial example, if we are going simply by the content of our experience, it is as obvious as anything can be that, at the end of my meal, I have the power to choose cake, or pie, or ice cream, or cookies, or nothing at all. Moreover, it is evident to the same degree that, if I have chosen pie, I could, at the moment I made that decision, have instead chosen cake, or ice cream, or nothing.

This last point is especially pertinent to the issue of moral responsibility. I reproach myself for having done something morally wrong precisely because, and only to the extent that, I sense that I could have done otherwise—I could have chosen to do the right thing instead. For if at the moment of action it was impossible for me to have done other than what I did, then how can I be held responsible for having done it, and deserve to be blamed and possibly punished as a consequence?

Some philosophers, called "compatibilists" or "soft determinists," will hold that I am still responsible for my action, and rightly blamed and punished for it, even if I couldn't at the moment of action have done otherwise, provided that no one else forced me to do what I did, that I did it, that I knew what I was doing when I did it, that I knew it was wrong when I did it, and that I did it because I wanted to, where this wanting flowed from my character, interests, and values. But the superficiality of this analysis is revealed as soon as we ask just *why* I had the character, interest, values, and desires that I had at the moment of action, and, for that matter, just why, at the moment of action, I couldn't have done otherwise than what I did. The answer will be that all of these things were determined—the necessary results of causal antecedents. And if that is right, then the idea that I am appropriately held responsible for my action, since it originated from me rather than from some external source, is shown to owe all of its plausibility to a simple failure to extend the logic of the relationship between agency and responsibility back far enough in the causal sequence. Everyone understands that I am not to blame if a sudden gust of wind picks me up and leaves me no choice but to fall on, and injure, an unsuspecting passerby. Why should the matter be any different if forces from my past that were every bit as much beyond my control as the gust of wind (say, my genetic inheritance and the way I was abused by caregivers in infancy) have rendered me now incapable of doing anything other than assaulting that same innocent passerby?

So perhaps the greatest weakness of the determinist hypothesis is that it contradicts our direct sense, in the moment of choosing, that it is entirely within our power to determine in which direction we will go. And it contradicts our sense of moral responsibility in accepting that we deserve to take the blame if the direction in which we choose to go is the wrong one. If determinism is true, these fundamental, universal, and frequently experienced intuitions are illusions. Indeed, even the determinists themselves tend to "admit the existence of an immediate consciousness of freedom." (BN, 79) By contrast, as Sartre pointed out, "determinism ... is not given as a reflective intuition," and so the "deterministic psychologists do not claim to found their thesis on the pure givens of introspection." (BN, 79) The best they can do, in defending their position, is to present it "as a satisfying hypothesis, the value of which comes from the fact that it accounts for the facts—or as a necessary postulate for establishing all psychology." (BN, 79)

While Sartre offered a few arguments against determinism, his main concern was not so much to refute it, as to offer a phenomenological description of freedom—that is, a description of what the experience of freedom is like, and of what is involved in the making of a free choice. Perhaps he proceeded in this way because he accepted Descartes' claim that freedom is "known without proof and merely by our experience of it." (CF, 528) True, he did occasionally append to his phenomenological descriptions arguments that are "transcendental," in Kant's sense. In these arguments he said, in effect, "our experience shows X, and the only possible way that could happen would be if we are free and determinism is false; therefore, we *are* free, and determinism *is* false."

But even if we do not accept those transcendental arguments, because we reject the premise that it would be impossible for determinism to produce the experiences in question, it is possible to construct on the basis of Sartre's phenomenological descriptions of freedom a less dogmatic but still powerful argument against determinism. For those descriptions add up to an account of freedom that is vastly more extensive, detailed, and vivid than any other ever offered in the history of philosophy, and they have the merit of demonstrating, to a degree that exceeds all previous accounts of the matter, how dramatically human actions differ from (any other kind of) events. (The point of the parentheses, here and in what follows, is to leave open the question of whether a human action is a kind of "event" that is merely very much unlike anything else that goes by that term, or whether it is so different as to belong to a different category entirely, so that it should not be considered an "event" at all.)

This goes to the issue of parsimony. Recall that the main argument for determinism is indirect. It is not the case that we experience the causes that supposedly necessitate the exact actions that we end up undertaking (quite the opposite); instead, the argument is that since we accept a causal account for everything else that happens, and since such an account would also be capable of explaining our actions, it seems either arbitrary or inconsistent to make those actions an exception to the general rule. Such a move, so the argument goes, offends against the principle of parsimony by multiplying assumptions unnecessarily, and by invoking two principles of explanation when one would be sufficient. But the more that human actions can be shown to differ from (other) events, and the more one therefore has to strain to fit both of them under the same singular explanatory framework, the less it will be an affront to the principle of parsimony to propose an alternative, non-deterministic, account of human actions—and this is especially so given that such an account is precisely the one that coheres with the data of our lived experience.

How, then, do actions differ from (other kinds of) events? Sartre discussed several differences, each of which can plausibly be regarded as essential and fundamental—a radical difference in kind, as opposed to a merely quantitative difference of degree.

For starters, notice that a genuine action (as opposed to a reflex—an automatic, instantaneous response to a stimulus) involves consciousness, an awareness of what one is doing, that is lacking in (other kinds of) events. In this way, the movements of my hands, mouth, jaws, and tongue as I engage in the act of eating a piece of blueberry pie differ dramatically in character from the movements of a leaf as it is gently blown through the air by the wind.

As a further point about parsimony, notice that there is nothing else in nature that is remotely like consciousness. And if consciousness exists, even though no one has a clue how this is possible, that is, no one understands how natural forces can somehow conspire to produce awareness and intentionality, then recognition of this might help to undercut the idea that it is extravagant to accept the idea that nature can also produce bodies capable of anti-deterministic freedom, however inexplicable that might seem to us at present. As a second difference, notice that actions, in stark contrast to (other kinds of) events, depend crucially on an agent's understanding of the meaning of a situation. Whereas the leaf moves away from a dog if the wind blows it in that direction, without the leaf's (nonexistent) interpretation of the situation affecting its movements even to the slightest degree, my action in either moving away from or toward the dog might depend almost entirely on whether I interpret its movements and expression as threatening, that is, as indicating a significant chance that it might attack and bite me if I were to approach it.

Thirdly, actions, unlike (other kinds of) events, can be understood teleologically—in terms of goals, or purposes. (Other kinds of) events admit only explanations that are completely mechanistic, rather than teleological. Again, when a leaf moves because it is being blown by the wind, neither it nor the wind is seeking any kind of end. The case is quite different when I cautiously move away from the snarling pit bull for the express purpose of avoiding being attacked by it.

Fourthly, precisely because of their teleological aspect, actions are oriented toward the future in a way that has no analogue in (other kinds of) events. The latter are caused by present forces, which, in turn, are the products of events that had taken place in the past. If I am not now playing tennis but am grabbing my racquet and heading for the courts in order to play, one can speculate about what precise combination of causal forces, bubbling up out of my past, may have joined forces to compel me to make the decision to go play tennis right now. But that *would* be speculation. What is certain is that my action is one that aims at a future that would be different from the present—a future in which I would be on the court, playing tennis. No such aiming at a different future is involved in a leaf moving through the air as it is blown by the wind.

Finally, and most importantly for Sartre, while (other kinds of) events can be explained entirely positively, in terms of existing things interacting with other existing things in accordance with the laws of physics (as when the wind blows a leaf through the air), actions always, and of necessity, introduce "negativities" into positive being.

Freedom and Negativity

This happens in several ways. Recall, first, that for Sartre consciousness is an activity, and every instance of perceiving, imagining, questioning, doubting, and so forth, is an *act* of consciousness. One result of his phenomenological investigations of consciousness is the finding that every act of consciousness in some sense denies, negates, or puts out of play some portion of positive being, and at the same time puts in play "negativities," that is, objects of experience, such as absences, meanings, and imaginaries, that have no positive, independent existence apart from the activities of consciousness. Indeed, consciousness is utterly unique because it is only with consciousness that "nothingness" is introduced into what would otherwise be purely positive being–hence the title of Sartre's magnum opus, *Being and Nothingness*.

This is significant since, according to Sartre, determinism holds sway only in the realm of positive being. Thus, consciousness by means of its ability to negate positive being, and to introduce negativities into it, is able radically to "disentangle" itself from, to become "unstuck" from, to avoid being "bogged down" in, the realm of positive being, and thereby evade its laws of deterministic causality. Several of Sartre's early philosophical writings, up to and including Part One and Part Two of *Being and Nothingness*, are largely devoted to the elaboration and clarification of that insight.

For example, in *The Imaginary* Sartre pointed out that an imagining consciousness focuses on things that are *not* present, *not* perceived, and often *not* existing, except as objects for an imagining consciousness. This shows that consciousness has the capacity to disengage with the causal order of positive beings, and to turn, instead, toward what is not. In this way, consciousness is utterly unlike a leaf, or the wind that blows it, both of which, in common with rocks and dirt and trees and gases, are mired in being, and capable only of confronting other positive beings. The peculiar and utterly unique ability of consciousness to call forth nonbeings suggests that it is not similarly "stuck." As Sartre put it, "for consciousness to be able to imagine, it must be able to escape from the world by its very nature, it must be able to stand back from the world by its own efforts. In a word, it must be free." (IM, 184) Thus, it is only "because we are transcendentally free that we can imagine." (IM, 186)

In *Being and Nothingness*, he made a similar argument in connection with another unique power of consciousness: the ability to ask questions. For notice that *things* are quite content to move along, bumping up against one another in conformity with deterministic laws of cause and effect, without ever asking why, or whether, they should do so. Consciousness's capacity for asking questions thus marks it as radically different from any kind of thing, just as the relation between a questioning consciousness and that which, or about which, it questions is unlike any kind of relation among things. Interrogation does resemble imagination, however, for in the same way that the act of imagining something requires a kind of standing back from being, and a kind of introduction of gaps, skips, or fissures into it, so does the act of asking a question. Accordingly, Sartre argued, in a manner parallel to his argument about imagination, that in asking a question it "is essential ... that the questioner have the permanent possibility of dissociating himself from the causal series which constitutes being and which can produce only being.... In so far as the questioner must be able to effect in relation to the questioned a kind of nihilating [that is, 'nothing-making'] withdrawal, he is not subject to the causal order of the world; he detaches himself from Being." (BN, 58)

And a similar argument holds for perception, since it, too, introduces negativities into being. The reason, as discussed in the previous chapter, is that perception requires selective focusing–that is, the elevation of some portion of one's perceptual field to the foreground, constituting it as a figure, and the simultaneous relegation of the remainder to a relatively undifferentiated, and only marginally noticed, background. Such focusing is necessary if one is to perceive anything specific at all since there is always a limitless abundance of things in one's perceptual field that might be noticed. The only way to pick out a "signal" among all that noise is to negate, to put out of action, a substantial portion of that perceptual field.

As perceptual fields do not organize themselves for us, and things do not dictate to us how they are to be focused on and conceptualized, these feats, which, once again, require the introduction of negativities into being, appear to be the accomplishments of free acts of consciousness. Moreover, insofar as one is conscious, there is a sense in which this freedom of focusing and of thought is omnipresent and inescapable. For one cannot be aware of anything without going beyond what is given by selectively attending to part of it (and doing so only in one of several possible ways) while nihilating the rest. This is one of the meanings of Sartre's oft-repeated claim that we are "condemned" to be free. And it is precisely because we are free in this sense that we typically encounter, in experience, a meaningful world rather than meaningless chaos.

Moreover, this freedom of focusing, in part because of its role in disclosing meanings, is foundational to freedom of choice. For, once again, the objects in our perceptual field do not affect us mechanistically. Rather, they must be interpreted and contextualized–that is, understood as meaningful elements in the "situation" that serves as the background against which we act. Thus, the factual state of affairs we confront can never, by itself, even *motivate* an action, let alone cause one. The reason is that one's interpretation of them as meaningful, and as comprising a situation, typically depends on one's projects, interests, and background knowledge, and these, in turn, require focusing acts of consciousness that negate and put entirely out of play many positive elements of one's perceptual field.

In Part Four of *Being and Nothingness*, and in his subsequent works, Sartre thickened and deepened his analysis of this foundational freedom of *consciousness* to focus, negate, interpret, and imagine, by expanding it to include the full-blooded freedom of embodied individuals to act on and to alter material conditions, economic and political structures, and other states of affairs that such agents confront in a social world that they share with others.

The starting point of Sartre's analysis was that "an action is on principle *intentional*." (BN, 559) When I genuinely *act*, I do so with purpose. And this entails a double negation. To act is to attempt to bring about something (a *desideratum*) that currently is not, and to reject or overturn what currently is. If I study, it is because I want to attain understanding and knowledge that I do not currently have, and thus to put an end to my current ignorance; if I take medicine, it is because I want to be well, and to overcome my present illness; if I turn on the air conditioner, it is because I want to be cool, and to overturn the unpleasantness of my current experience of feeling hot; and so on endlessly.

But Sartre insisted that no objective facts pertaining to me, such as my ignorance, illness, or discomfort from feeling hot, are capable, all by themselves, to cause me to take an action. Rather, I must "color" those objectivities "with insufficiency," taking them as conditions to be transcended, if they are to serve as the basis for my action.

And the same analysis holds for the social, economic, historical, and political structures in which we find ourselves immersed, often against our will. Sartre offered the example of a worker whose salary is low. This objective fact cannot motivate an action of revolt if the worker thinks of his or her salary simply in positive terms, as a certain number of dollars per week. What is required, instead, is for the worker to evaluate the salary negatively, as "insufficient," "not enough," "unfair," or "unjust." Such a worker "will have to have effected a double nihilation: on the one hand, he must posit an ideal state of affairs as a pure present nothingness; on the other hand, he must posit the actual situation as nothingness in relation to this state of affairs." From this analysis Sartre drew two conclusions: "(1) No factual state whatever it may be ... is capable by itself of motivating any act whatsoever. For an act is a projection ... toward what is not, and what is can in no way determine by itself what is not. (2) No factual state can determine consciousness to apprehend it as a [negativity] or as a lack." (BN, 562)

Anguish

But, according to Sartre, we need not rely solely on such indirect arguments in order to achieve knowledge of our own freedom; for when consciousness reflectively takes itself for an object, it is able to stare its own freedom in the face. Sartre's name for this phenomenon, a reflective consciousness of freedom, is "anguish."

In order to clarify the nature of anguish, Sartre distinguished it from fear. I experience fear when I am worried about an external threat. Sartre offered the following example. Suppose I am walking high in the mountains and suddenly find myself at the edge of an abyss with no guardrail. Recognizing that an external force, such as a sudden gust of wind or a slight shifting of the dirt or rocks beneath my feet, could cause me to plunge to my death, I am fearful.

But now suppose that I respond to my fearful situation by resolving to proceed slowly and extremely cautiously, paying careful attention with each step to the wind, to the dirt and rocks underfoot, and to every other potentially dangerous element in my environment. While it might be the case, and I might recognize it to be so, that the consistent adoption of such precautions would indeed be adequate to shield me from danger, a new worry emerges. How can I be sure now that I will stick to my resolution to the end? For it occurs to me that I am frequently guilty of both carelessness and overconfidence. In the light of that, how can I know at this moment that after having successfully walked for some distance along the edge of the abyss without incident I will not relax, let down my guard, and believe that this situation is not as difficult or as dangerous as I had initially thought? How can I be sure that I will continue to proceed with the required caution, and to attend to my dangerous surroundings with adequate care? My new worry is not that I am uncertain that such precautions will be effective, but rather, as Sartre put it, that I am uncertain "that they will be adopted." (BN, 67) In other words, my concern is now directed toward my own future conduct, rather than to any external threat. This is anguish.

This example illustrates yet another way in which conscious actions are, from the outset, rooted in negativity. For what the phenomenon of anguish reveals, according to Sartre, is that conscious agents differ radically from nonconscious things in that their very being is characterized by ambiguity and negation. While nonconscious things, in conformity with the logical principle of identity, simply are what they are, conscious agents are what they are only in a limited sense and to a limited degree (hence the ambiguity), and in another sense are precisely not "what they are" (hence the negation).

To see this, consider my relation, at the moment at which I resolve to exercise maximum caution while walking in the mountains, to the walker I am counting on to keep this resolution. Is that walker me? In one sense, the answer would appear obviously to be "yes." After all, it is clearly not someone else, as my worry would be of a different character if it were. But it is clear that in at least two respects the future walker is not me. First, I am temporally separated from him. Secondly, and far more importantly, for that reason, his conduct is beyond my present control. Sartre, who seemed to enjoy paradoxical formulations, summarized the results of this analysis this way: "I am what I am not, and am not what I am." Or, to be more precise, "*I am the self which I will be, in the mode of not being it.*" (BN, 68) "Anguish," then, "is precisely my consciousness of being my own future, in the mode of not-being," since "the decisive conduct will emanate from a self which I am not yet...." (BN, 68-9)

One finds this same separation and negation, this same failure to coincide with oneself, when we shift our focus from the moment in which I make a resolution to that in which I am called upon to carry it out. Here we are moving from a consideration of anguish in the face of the future—the kind in which, as Sartre put it, I make an appointment with myself and then worry that I won't show up to keep the appointment (BN, 73)—to that of anguish in the face of the past. Sartre's example is that of a gambler who has freely and sincerely resolved not to gamble anymore. Confident that his resolution has ended his gambling, and that the issue is now settled, he

Freedom | 77

is horrified to find, when he approaches the gaming table, that he must confront "in anguish" the "total inefficacy of the past resolution."

The problem, once again, is a failure of self-identity. Whereas a nonconscious thing is identical to the sum of its properties, and exhausts itself in being that collection of properties, the gambler's property of "not-gambling," which he had attempted to attach to himself by means of a resolution, is something of which he is conscious. To the precise extent that he is conscious *of* it, that it is an object *for* his consciousness, he is not identical with it, but rather surpasses it.

> What the gambler apprehends at this instant is again the permanent rupture in determinism; it is nothingness which separates him from himself; I should have liked so much not to gamble anymore; yesterday I even had a synthetic apprehension of the situation (threatening ruin, disappointment of my relatives) as *forbidding me* to play. It seemed to me that I had established a *real barrier* between gambling and myself, and now I suddenly perceive that my former understanding of the situation is no more than a memory of an idea, a memory of a feeling. In order for it to come to my aid once more, I must remake it *ex nihilo* [that is, out of nothing] and freely. The not-gambling is only one of my possibilities, as the fact of gambling is another of them, neither more nor less. *I must rediscover* the fear of financial ruin or of disappointing my family, etc., I must re-create it as experienced fear. It stands behind me like a boneless phantom. It depends on me alone to lend it flesh. I am alone and naked before temptation as I was the day before. After having patiently built up barriers and walls, after enclosing myself in the magic circle of a resolution, I perceive with anguish that *nothing* prevents me from gambling. (BN, 70)

This point about my consciousness of my past resolutions can be generalized. It applies equally well to anything else with which I might be identified, including my "ego," my personality, my interests and dispositions, my motives, and all of the "facticities" that characterize me at present, such as my age, height, weight, color, occupation, nationality, social role, and so forth. By focusing on these things, I put myself at a distance from them. I cannot simply *be* any of these things since they are objects *for* me. They are like the objects in my perceptual field in that they neither announce their meaning to me, nor organize themselves into a situation for my benefit, nor dictate to me how I am to respond to them. Rather, they become meaningful only as I undertake projects on the basis of them or in spite of them, and thus surpass them in reaching toward some end. Should I wish to escape my freedom and responsibility by allowing my personality, or character, or motives, or resolutions to determine for me what I am to do, I will discover, in anguish, that these objects for my consciousness invariably refuse to perform this function for me, but instead always refer me back to my own freedom. Sartre did not draw this conclusion on the basis of a transcendental argument or any other kind of inference. Rather, he offered it as a descriptive, phenomenological account of the data of lived experience. There is no escaping the unending task of having to choose, and of having to take responsibility for those choices.

Sartre acknowledged no exceptions whatsoever to this rule. No set of circumstances can rob a conscious agent of his or her freedom since no factual state can determine all by itself what action will be undertaken in response to it. Every factual state can accommodate an indefinite number of actions and can be apprehended as deficient, as "to be transcended," in multiple ways. Every set of objective circumstances is capable of serving as the background against which a variety of projects might be launched. Every state of affairs permits a choice of action. Accordingly, Sartre drew the conclusion, which is often criticized as "extreme" and "outrageous"–that we are "absolutely free," (BN, 653) "totally free," (BN, 709) "wholly and forever free," (BN, 569) and "condemned to be free," (BN, 567, 653, 673, 707) and that "the slave in chains," therefore, "is as free as his master." (BN, 703)

Freedom as Necessarily Situated

But this obviously does not mean that I can "choose to be tall if I am short," or "to have two arms if I have only one." (BN, 619) Rather, Sartre consistently maintained that "I am never free except *in situation*," (BN, 653) that "*being situated* is an essential and necessary characteristic of freedom," (WIL, 133) and that "being-in-situation defines human reality." (BN, 702)

This raises the question of what Sartre meant by "situation." One might suppose that my situation is reducible to my facticity (that is, the objective facts about me and my environment as they exist in a particular time and place). But that can't be right, since a situation is meaningful, and, as we have noted, Sartre repeatedly pointed out that meaning can only arise when something objective is transcended and illuminated by the activity of a free consciousness engaged in a project. So my situation is the result of the confrontation between my facticity and my free consciousness. As he put it, "the situation is neither objective nor subjective," and "can be considered neither as the free result of a freedom nor as the ensemble of the constraints to which I am subject; it stems from the illumination of the constraint by freedom which gives to it its meaning as constraint." (BN, 704)

Sartre gave the example of a crag that one encounters in the countryside, (BN, 620, 627-29) which might be immediately perceived (variously, depending on one's projects and interests) as, for example, "a big, heavy thing that is in the way and needs to be removed," as "a tall thing to climb so as to get a good look at the countryside," or as "a beautiful thing that will add a lot of interest to the landscape painting I plan to execute." The point, once again, is that we never encounter brute facticity as such, but rather we always see it only as it is colored by our freely chosen projects, and through a selective focus that highlights just some of the elements in our perceptual field while relegating others to a relatively undifferentiated and only marginally noticed, if not entirely ignored, background.

It must be emphasized, however, that there is an involuntary dimension to our uncovering of the "brute existent." Though it is only by means of our selective focusing that meanings can come to light, those meanings are also constrained by the nature of what is objectively present. Unlike a tall crag, a deep ditch cannot be encountered as a thing "to be climbed, so as to achieve a vantage point from which to view the countryside." The objective properties of things can facilitate–and even suggest–some projects, even as they render others difficult, and still others impossible. So the "absolute" and inescapable freedom of which Sartre spoke is a freedom to select from among the meanings and projects that the objective facts will accommodate, not a freedom to alter those facts at will, as if by magic.

Thus, if I am short (to return to an example mentioned at the outset of this section), I am free to undertake a variety of projects against the background of that fact. I might choose to become a jockey or enter into some other profession in which my small stature would work to my advantage. Or I might attempt to achieve great wealth and fame, in the hope that people would tend to notice these marks of distinction rather than my height. Or I might wear elevator shoes. Or I might simply attempt to cultivate an attitude of indifference about my height, and one of contempt for those who would judge me negatively because of it. While these projects admit of a possibility of being carried out with some degree of success, the project of simply "being tall," by the mere act of wishing it or choosing it, obviously does not. Sartre, as much as anyone, was perfectly aware of that.

But if freedom is always situated, and if its character as such means that it always faces obstacles, limitations, and restrictions, then why did Sartre continue to call this freedom "absolute?" Similarly, if the "always situated" nature of freedom means that there are always a great number of projects that are closed off to it entirely, why did he nonetheless insist that such prohibitions do not diminish its character as freedom? Sartre's answer is that "the resistance which freedom reveals in the existent ... results only in enabling it to arise as freedom. There can be [freedom] only as engaged in a resisting world. Outside of this engagement the notion ... of freedom ... loses all meaning." (BN, 621)

Sartre's point was that there would be no freedom in a world that offered no resistance, but rather yielded whatever we want at the very moment that we want it. Freedom can only be meaningful for beings with finite power, who can't have everything all at once, and who therefore must make choices. In the world as it is, one must choose, for example, between eating rich desserts constantly and maintaining a trim figure. There would be no need for choice, and thus no point to freedom, if one could, simply and effortlessly, have both at the same time. As Sartre put it, "freedom can exist only as *restricted* since freedom is choice. Every choice... supposes elimination and selection; every choice is a choice of finitude." (BN, 636) Thus,

> The very project of a freedom in general is a choice which implies the anticipation and acceptance of some kind of resistance somewhere. Not only does freedom constitute the compass within which [nonconscious things] otherwise indifferent will be revealed as resistances, but freedom's very project in general is to *do* in a resisting world by means of a victory over the world's resistances. (BN, 650)

Two Senses of "Freedom"

Perhaps the foregoing is sufficient to refute the notion that Sartre, in maintaining that we are always "absolutely free," was endorsing the preposterous idea that we are free to choose anything, at any time, with no restrictions, so that I can simply choose to be tall if I am short, or to see if I am blind. As we have seen, his view, quite to the contrary, is that freedom is *always* situated, *always* encounters resistances, and *always* finds itself in circumstances that would absolutely preclude the making of certain choices. But the fact that every set of circumstances also does permit the making of other choices, and thus not only allows but *requires* the exercise of freedom, was the basis for Sartre's controversial claim that everyone, everywhere, is always free. This, however, gives rise to a different, extremely widespread, criticism. If everyone, everywhere, at every time, is *absolutely* free, how are we to make sense of the seemingly obvious truth that some states of affairs are more conducive to freedom than others, and, consequently, that some people, such as slaves and prisoners, are *less* free than others?

In anticipation of this criticism, Sartre in *Being and Nothingness* drew a distinction between, on the one hand, "the empirical and popular concept of freedom," which amounts to "the ability to obtain the ends chosen," and, on the other hand, "the technical and philosophical concept of freedom," which "means only the autonomy of choice." (BN, 621-22; see also BN, 648) This distinction allowed him to acknowledge that slaves and prisoners are significantly less free than the rest of us with regard to their "freedom of obtaining," even as he continued to maintain that their "freedom of choice" is absolute and equivalent to our own. (BN, 622)

But many of Sartre's critics, overlooking this distinction, have scolded him for allegedly denying, by implication, that anyone is oppressed or needs to be liberated (since, after all, everyone is already "absolutely free"). In an essay published in 1944, just a year after the appearance of *Being and Nothingness*, Sartre responded to such critics as follows:

> You call us social traitors, saying that our conception of freedom keeps man from loosening his chains. What stupidity! When we say a man who's out of work is free, we don't mean that he can do whatever he wants and change himself into a rich and tranquil bourgeois on the spot. *He is free because he*

> can always choose to accept his lot with resignation or to rebel against it. (MPCE, 159)

In a 1946 essay he made a similar point: "But, say the Marxists, if you teach man that he is free, you betray him; for he no longer needs to *become* free; can you conceive of a man free from birth who demands to be liberated? To this I reply that if man is not originally free, but determined once and for all, we cannot even conceive what his liberation might be." (MAR, 244) And a major theme of his *Notebooks for an Ethics* is that "only a freedom can be oppressed," because "if we pretend that man is not free, the very idea of oppression loses all meaning." After all, "[a] stone does not oppress, [and] one does not oppress a stone." (NFE, 327)

These passages suggest that freedom of choice and freedom of obtaining, while distinct, are connected to one another. The former is foundational to the latter. Freedom of choice (that is, freedom from determinism) is a necessary, but not a sufficient, condition for freedom of obtaining (that is, political and economic freedom, and especially freedom from oppression and exploitation). Freedom of choice is a necessary condition for freedom of obtaining, because a being subject to thoroughgoing determinism would not be "free" even if no one oppressed it and all of its needs and desires were met. But it is not a sufficient condition, because a being with "absolute" freedom of choice might yet be unfree in the sense that it is enslaved or otherwise oppressed, and/or it is unable to meet even its most basic and essential needs.

In Sartre's later career, as he devoted more and more attention to social, political, and economic issues, there was a corresponding increase in his engagement with freedom of obtaining. For example, in a 1960 interview, he asserted that "freedom–not metaphysical but practical freedom–is conditioned by proteins. Life will be human on the day that everyone can eat his fill and every man can work at a job under suitable working conditions." (As quoted in CR, 387) Similarly, he endorsed the notion of a "concrete freedom," which would mean "the right to have more than one pair of shoes and to eat when one is hungry" (WSR, 453), and speaks of the need *"for everyone"* to have "a margin of *real* freedom beyond the production of life." (SFM 34)

The Slave in Chains

Sartre's distinction between two senses of freedom also helps us to understand his much-criticized claim that the slave in chains is as free as his master. Clearly, he did not mean by this anything as morally obtuse as that the slave's life is as good as the master's, that the range of options open to the slave is as rich and varied as the master's, that the slave has the same access to the good things of life as does the master, or that the slave is free in the sense of not being oppressed or standing in need of liberation. To think otherwise would be to confuse practical freedom (freedom of obtaining) with ontological freedom (freedom of choice).

But this raises a new worry. Given how horrible the slave's condition is, and how little freedom of obtaining he or she has, surely the "absolute" freedom that Sartre attributed to the slave must be a trivial one. Any freedom of the slave's that is equal to our own must be an inconsequential inner freedom, that is, a freedom of attitude, of desiring, of judging, and of wishing. But Sartre explicitly rejected such an "inner freedom," calling it "a pure idealist hoax," on the grounds that "care is taken never to present it as the necessary condition of the *act*." (MAR, 237) Instead, he insisted that freedom of choice, the absolute, inalienable freedom of slaves (and of everyone else) is neither "a license to do whatever one wants" nor an "internal refuge that would remain to us even in our chains." (WIL, 264) For such a freedom

> supposes a commencement of realization in order that the choice may be distinguished from the dream and the wish. Thus we shall not say that a prisoner is always free to go out

Freedom | 85

of prison, which would be absurd, nor that he is always free to long for release, which would be an irrelevant truism, but that he is always free to try to escape...; that is, that whatever his condition may be, he can project his escape and learn the value of his project by undertaking some action. (BN, 622)

So the point of Sartre's claim was simply that slaves, no less than the rest of us, including their masters, but in total contrast to stones, must give meaning to their facticity by surpassing it. They can (and must) make choices—including choices about how best to cope with their situation as slaves, and, more fundamentally, about whether to accept their lot as slaves or to engage instead in a project of revolt. The oppressed of all kinds, no less than their oppressors, must ask: "What shall I do?" What is important to me?" "What do I stand for?"

Nor should Sartre's insistence that even slaves have freedom of choice, and are responsible for how they respond to their objective circumstances, be construed as insensitivity to the horrors of oppression, or to the immorality of the oppressors, or to the responsibility of the oppressors for their acts of oppression. To the contrary, few authors have ever shown such sustained concern for the plight of the oppressed, or have condemned as harshly the acts of oppressors of all kinds, or have so annoyed so many members of the privileged classes by exposing and decrying their apathetic indifference to the suffering of the poor. In *Anti-Semite and Jew* he addressed this issue directly: "The prisoner is always free to run away, if it is clearly understood that he risks death in crawling under the barbed wire. Is his jailor any less guilty on that account." (ASJ, 136)

Sartre's writings make quite clear his understanding that some objective circumstances impose hardships. Such conditions as being enslaved, or subjected to constant physical abuse, or being blind, or unable to walk, or unemployed, or homeless, or ill, or desperately poor, limit possibilities, stand in the way of the realization of certain important values, and diminish one's chances of successfully carrying out various valuable projects. So it is obvious that such conditions are bad, and are to be avoided if possible. But it is not clear that the long list of ways in which such things are bad should include the charge that they diminish freedom of choice. For if I am blind, for example, I still must decide which projects to undertake within the range of possibilities that condition can accommodate. The general point is that "to be free is not to choose the historic world in which one arises—which would have no meaning—but to choose oneself in the world whatever this may be." (BN, 668) That is a task that everyone, equally, must face.

5. Sartre's Legacy

As controversial as Sartre was in life, so he remains in death. There is no consensus as regards his lasting influence and significance. On the one hand, many of the French philosophers who have risen to prominence in the period following his death did their best to see that he remains buried. Typical of these is Jean Baudrillard, who casually dismissed Sartre's philosophy as passé, remarking, "Who cares about freedom, bad faith, and authenticity today?" (JB, 73)

But on the other hand, Patrick Baert, in a recent study, provided evidence that Sartre remains a potent force in contemporary French culture:

> Sartre still frequently pops up on France Culture, the French radio station devoted to intellectual and cultural matters. In the last three years, for instance, France culture aired his play *Les Mouches*, plus five other major programmes *solely* devoted to him. Both Sartre's persona and oeuvre are still regularly discussed and revisited on the literary pages of *Le Monde*, *Libération* and *Le Figaro*, ... prompted ... often by the appearance of new, weighty academic works. [Annie] Cohen-Solal's latest book, *Une Renaissance sartrienne*, is a recent example ..., and indeed widely discussed. (PB, 156-57)

Nor is this interest in Sartre confined to France. The notable American literary critic Fredric Jameson, in a 2016 essay, made a strong case for the contemporary (and continuing) relevance and importance of Sartre's ideas:

> I can testify that younger readers are still electrified by the descriptions of *Being and Nothingness* and readily acknowledge the phenomenological and philosophical truth of its accounts of freedom.... [T]he *Transcendence of the Ego*, ...

[with] its displacement of the 'self' and of personal identity ...is still very much with us today.... Those pages of the *Critique [of Dialectical Reason]* ... in which Sartre contrasts the small-group dynamics of guerilla or nomadic units with the serial alienation of larger public-opinion-type collectives, still have an unparalleled urgency, both political and philosophical, today.... [T]oday, it is not particularly the notion of class struggle that needs reviving: we see it inescapably everywhere around us. What we need is some renewed awareness of what class consciousness itself is and how it functions.... Sartre ... has significant things to tell us about that. (FJ, 127-128, 131)

And Ronald Aronson, in an essay in the *New York Times* commemorating the centenary of Sartre's birth, argued that:

Today Sartre is still as troubling and annoying as ever. He demands that we see a world seemingly out of control as made up of human choices and the structures these create. When he demands that we take responsibility for our lives, for the shape of our world, for the situation of the least favored—for others as well as ourselves—he is expressing decisively important conditions for learning to live as responsible citizens in this globalized world. This is no outmoded radicalism, but the message of one of the most challenging and contemporary philosophies. (RA)

Little wonder, then, that books, both scholarly and popular (Sarah Bakewell's *At the Existentialist Cafe: Freedom, Being, and Apricot Cocktails*, published in 2016, was an international best-seller), articles, and dissertations on Sartre continue to appear every year; that his works are still assigned in college courses; that some of his plays (most notably *No Exit*) continue to be staged; and that scholarly societies devoted to his work—organizations that hold conferences and, in some cases, publish journals—remain active in Great Britain,

Brazil, Italy, Japan, and the United States and Canada, in addition to France.

World events have unwittingly conspired to attract renewed interest in Sartre's political theorizing, which had been widely ridiculed and despised during his lifetime. In our world, unlike the one in which he lived and wrote, capitalism reigns supreme everywhere, un-threatened by any serious challenger. What is the result? The gap separating rich from poor widens every year; the use of torture as an interrogation technique is on the rise; governmental surveillance of ordinary citizens is becoming routine; an amorphous "war on terror" continues to rage with no apparent end in sight; and the accelerating increase in global temperatures threatens to put an end to human life on the planet. In light of these trends, millions are searching for an alternative both to the prevailing capitalist order and to the murderous tyrannies of the 20th century that called themselves anti-capitalist. Sartre's various attempts to fuse selected Marxist insights (about the contradictions of capitalism, the reality of economic and social structures as forces in the direction of history, and the importance of coordinated group activity in the production of progressive political change) with his own analyses of individual consciousness, freedom, and responsibility, thus stand before us as a highly promising, and underutilized, resource.

In the concluding paragraph of John Gerassi's biography of Sartre, he offered the opinion that "From 1945 on, Sartre did more than any other intellectual in the world to denounce injustice and to support the wretched of the earth." (GER, 187) Sartre's continuing relevance is partly attributable to the fact that the injustices he denounced are still very much with us. Indeed, his work has helped to inspire contemporary political activist movements, such as Occupy Wall Street (several books by and about him were included in its "People's Library") and Black Lives Matter.

His enduring relevance is also evidenced by his continuing widespread influence on popular culture and the arts. In this connection, one can cite such otherwise diverse works as the plays of Harold

Pinter, the films of Woody Allen, the recordings of Pink Floyd, and the television show *The Good Place*.

Pinter, recipient of the 2005 Nobel Prize in Literature, deals with Sartrean existentialist themes, such as the modern tendency to respond inauthentically to the burdens associated with freedom, responsibility, and the need to create meaning for oneself, in several of his early plays, including *The Birthday Party*, *The Caretaker*, and *A Slight Ache*. Later plays, including *The Hothouse*, *Precisely*, *One for the Road*, *Mountain Language*, and *The New World Order*, expose and criticize the horrors of contemporary politics—authoritarianism, the suspension of human rights, the use of torture—in a manner that is reminiscent, both in terms of style and substance, of Sartre's political plays. It is noteworthy, in this connection, that Pinter appeared as an actor in a famous BBC production of *No Exit*, portraying Garcin, the central male character.

Allen has cited Sartre as one of his favorite authors. One of Sartre's books is depicted in his film *Husbands and Wives*; another is featured in *Anything Else*; and a book collection drawn from the *Inside Woody Allen* comic strip, written by Allen, is titled *Non-Being and Something-Ness*—an obvious spoof of Sartre's *Being and Nothingness*. Allen dramatized Sartrean ideas in several of his movies. *Zelig*, the story of a man possessed of a spectacular ability to blend in with any crowd, powerfully presents the existentialist critique of inauthenticity, showing how, in politics, it facilitates fascism. And another Sartrean concern, the need for personal responsibility and the creation of meaning in a Godless, amoral cosmos, is a recurring theme in Allen's films, perhaps most evident in *Crimes and Misdemeanors* and *Match Point*. (See IPI and PF)

The music of Pink Floyd, especially in the sequence of albums beginning with *The Dark Side of the Moon*, continuing through *Wish You Were Here* and *Animals*, and concluding with *The Wall*, is largely devoted to exploring what Sartre, in *Existentialism is a Humanism*, called our "thrown" condition—that is, the fact that we find ourselves already immersed in a world full of existential, economic, political, and cultural structures that we have not chosen, but to which we must nonetheless respond. These albums fully endorse, and amplify, the Sartrean thesis that our responsibility to respond to such structures is both inescapable and grave. In *Dark Side*, for example, successive songs treat our responsibility to deal with the pressures imposed on us by time, finitude, death, the struggle to make money, and the necessity of living cooperatively with people who differ from us. (See DDS)

The Good Place, a highly acclaimed NBC television series that ran four seasons from 2016-2020, deals with philosophical issues, especially within the domain of ethics. Set in the afterlife, one of the central characters is a deceased philosophy professor, who provides instruction in ethics to another character, who is engaged in the project of trying to become a good person so that she will deserve to be in "The Good Place." At the conclusion of the show's first season, we learn that "The Good Place" is actually a bad place, and that the four souls dwelling there had been chosen for it precisely on the basis of their potential to torture one another—an idea rather obviously derived from Sartre's *No Exit*. Series creator and executive producer Michael Schur, in a presentation to the 2018 annual meeting of the North American Sartre Society, confirmed his show's indebtedness to Sartre, not only for its central premise, but also for several other philosophical ideas addressed in its various episodes.

Sartre's cultural status is further indicated by his enduring presence in the world of satire, from Monty Python, in the famous sketch, "Mrs. Premise and Mrs. Conclusion Visit Jean-Paul Sartre," to *Saturday Night Live* in a segment spoofing a detective show, "Sartresky & Hutch"—the announcer, speaking of the two detectives, informs us that "one's tough; the other is existential." Then there is also the animated series, *Rick and Morty* (in which the 14-year-old Morty declares, "Nobody exists on purpose, nobody belongs anywhere, everybody's gonna die").

Or consider the following entry on Sartre, from a comic article based on a premise of pretending that great writers had been baseball players:

All-star Cincinnati shortstop Johnny P. Sartre in 1964 became the first major leaguer to refuse the Most Valuable Player Award. Sartre declined the prestigious award because of his long-standing opposition to the infield-fly rule. He denounced the rule, claiming that it severely limited human freedom and that it introduced into the game "a momentary paralysis in the midst of movement—all play suddenly assumes an automatic quality." The lifetime .350 hitter had made news several years earlier when he referred to the Ground Rule Double as an "absurd bourgeois convention." (GM)

Though he no doubt would not have hated it, Sartre even maintained a presence in the world of advertising. A double-page advertisement for Microsoft's *Encarta* multimedia encyclopedia that appeared in *Vanity Fair* depicts two young girls under the headline, "Forget Goldilocks and the Three Bears, tell us about Sartre." The ad continues: "'C'mon, dad, tell us about Sartre and existentialism and his belief in the inescapable responsibility of all individuals for their own decisions and his relationship with Simone de Beauvoir,' we pleaded as he tucked us in for the night." The ad goes on to report that the father dutifully complies, loading the encyclopedia into his computer and calling up the entry on Sartre. "After he kissed us goodnight," the ad continues, "Dad said Sartre was fond of saying, 'Man is condemned to be free.' We told him he was free to keep us up as long as he wanted with stories about Sartre. He chuckled, turned out the lights, and said, 'I think you two have had enough existentialism for one night.'" (GC, 278)

It is ironic that Sartre's thought should prove so enduring, given that he had described, in *Search for a Method*, a future in which "existentialism will no longer have any reason for being." (SFM, 181) However, since this prophecy was conditioned on the future realization of a world in which "there will exist for everyone a margin of *real* freedom beyond the production of life," (SFM, 34) it seems likely that Sartre will remain with us for quite some time.

Suggested Reading

Sartre was a remarkably prolific writer, having authored over 600 works, and in a wide variety of genres. It would be impossible to discuss all of them in this short book. However, as a guide to further reading, I offer the following list of what I take to be his 50 most interesting and/or important works. I will provide bibliographical information for each work on my list, as well as a few remarks on its content. These annotations will also allow me to expand on some of the issues discussed in earlier chapters, and to introduce briefly a few others not treated there.

1. **Imagination** (1936), trans. Kenneth Williford and David Rudrauf (New York: Routledge, 2012). There is also a translation by Forrest Williams (Ann Arbor: University of Michigan Press, 1972).

This was Sartre's first book. It is mostly devoted to criticism of several prominent modern philosophical and psychological theories of the imagination. Of greatest interest is the book's concluding section, in which he offers a sympathetic account of Edmund Husserl's phenomenological approach to the topic.

2. **The Transcendence of the Ego** (1937), trans. Forrest Williams and Robert Kirkpatrick (New York: Hill and Wang, 1991). There is also a translation by Andrew Brown (New York: Routledge, 2004).

It was in this work that Sartre presented his argument, discussed at length in Chapter Three above, that there is no pre-existing ego or "self" inhabiting or underlying consciousness. He claimed that the ego is not a substance, directing consciousness, but rather a construct, an object *for* consciousness, that consciousness brings into being by selectively synthesizing several of its own reflective acts.

    3. **"The Wall"** (1937), in *The Wall and Other Stories*, trans. Lloyd Alexander (New York: New Directions, 1975).

This was the first short story that Sartre published as an adult. It received rapturous reviews upon publication and helped to establish Sartre as a major writer. It has taken on the status of a classic in the short story genre, having been reprinted in countless anthologies, and made into a movie in 1967.

    Written in response to the Spanish Civil War, it is a tense, suspenseful, atmospheric account of the experiences of a prisoner of war during what he believes to be his final night of life before being executed in the morning.

    4. ***Nausea*** (1938), trans. Robert Baldick (Harmondsworth, Middlesex, England: Penguin, 2000). There is also a translation by Lloyd Alexander (New York: New Directions, 2013).

This was Sartre's first novel. Published right on the heels of "The Wall," its reception cemented Sartre's literary reputation and established that his mastery extended to long-form fiction. Some of the ideas it presents are discussed in Chapter Three.

    One additional theme not addressed above is the difference between life and art. Life, as it is lived, is messy, and full of superfluous, irrelevant detail. If something interesting happened to you while you were walking down a street today, an account of that event that failed to discriminate between what was relevant to it, and interesting and important, and what was not, would go on forever, and the experience of hearing or reading such an account would be intolerably boring. Suppose that the point of interest in your experience while walking down the street was the fact that you bumped into an old friend who lives overseas, and who you have not seen in thirty years. Such facts as that you were wearing brown shoes at the time, that the laces of each shoe were 27 inches long, that you had taken 19 steps on Boylston Street when you first spotted your friend, that you were feeling slightly thirsty at the time, and so on forever, would be utterly irrelevant to the story, and, in part for that reason, uninteresting. If you are a good storyteller, or even merely a minimally competent one, you will leave these details out when you tell others about this reunion. Similarly, fictional stories, that is, literary works of art, are ruthlessly selective in what they include and what they leave out. They do not ramble on pointlessly, but rather stick to what is essential and necessary to their artistic purpose. Stories and plays, and, for that matter, pieces of music, have a logic and structure to them that is lacking in life as it is lived. Stories and songs typically have clear beginnings and endings. Life does not. It just keeps on going. Observing this, Roquentin, the novel's protagonist, remarks in his diary, "I wanted moments of my life to follow one another in an orderly fashion like those of a life remembered. You might as well try to catch time by the tail." (N, 63)

In *Nausea*, the work of art that is discussed extensively in this context is a song, "Some of These Days." Every note of its melody is necessary and essential. To change even one note would alter, and diminish, the tune. Moreover, the melody is indestructible, for it is distinguishable from any performance of it, or recording of it, or written representation of it in sheet music. It is untouched by the scratchy imperfections of the one particular copy of one recording that Roquentin hears (a good listener is able, in his or her auditory experience, to push such noise into the background so as to focus solely on the "signal," that is the music). Thus, art is capable of achieving a kind of perfection, timelessness, purity, and precision that no human life could ever hope to match. Accordingly, at the end of *Nausea*, Roquentin ponders the idea that he might be able to justify, and find meaning in, his otherwise seemingly pointless existence by creating art. So he resolves to write a novel.

There is some evidence that Sartre, at the time when he wrote *Nausea*, shared Roquentin's vision of the creation of art as a means to personal salvation. If so, he definitely abandoned it later on in favor of the view that writing was more about a free exchange of ideas among writers and readers, and about their joining together in a project of attempting to disclose truths about the world, and to bring about, on the basis of such knowledge, needed social, political, and economic changes. Commenting in a 1964 interview on how much his views had changed since the time of *Nausea*, he remarked, "what I lacked [then] was a sense of reality. I have changed since. I have slowly learned to experience reality. I have seen children dying of hunger. Over against a dying child *Nausea* cannot act as a counterweight." (LBSM, 62)

5. **"The Childhood of a Leader"** (1939), in *The Wall and Other Stories*.

This story recounts the adventures of a confused and insecure young man who, in an attempt to win the respect of others and to gain for himself a sense of his own identity, attempts to "be" a fascist and anti-Semite. This well-constructed and entertaining story introduces several themes that Sartre would develop in greater detail in later, nonfiction, works. These include, most prominently, bad faith (*Being and Nothingness*), anti-Semitism (*Anti-Semite and Jew*), and the psychology of the fascist mentality (several political writings).

6. ***Sketch for a Theory of the Emotions*** (1939), trans. Philip Mairet (New York: Routledge, 2014). It has also been translated by Bernard Frechtman as *The Emotions: Outline of a Theory* (New York: The Wisdom Library, 1948).

In this short book, Sartre offered a phenomenological account of emotional experience. He attempted to show that the popular conception of emotion as a state, something that we *have* and passively endure, is wrong. Emotions are more accurately characterized as modes of awareness of the world. They are neither projections in consciousness of disturbances in the body nor involuntary, reflex, reactions to external stimuli, but rather intentional conscious acts–prereflective responses to meanings (for example, "threatening," "horrible," or "wonderful") encountered in experience.

7. **"A Fundamental Idea of Husserl's Phenomenology: Intentionality,"** in *Critical Essays*, trans. Chris Turner (New York: Seagull Books, 2017). It is also available in *We Have Only This Life to Live: The Selected Essays of Jean-Paul Sartre 1939-1975*, ed. Ronald Aronson and Adrian van den Hoven (New York: New York Review Books, 2013).

This short essay helped to introduce Husserl's phenomenology to a French audience. In it, Sartre defended the idea, discussed in Chapter Three, that consciousness is not a *thing*, a *container* that takes ideas into itself, but rather an *activity* of reaching out toward and focusing on external objects. Sartre gave to this seemingly dry and technical thesis a highly dramatic treatment, and suggested that it entails consequences of enormous importance.

8. **"Monsieur François Mauriac and Freedom"** (1939), in *Critical Essays*. A different translation, titled "François Mauriac and Freedom," can be found in *Literary and Philosophical Essays*, trans. Annette Michelson (New York: Collier Books, 1962).

Aside from lengthy, more general and theoretical works, such as *What is Literature?*, this is the most famous of Sartre's many works of literary criticism. It is a bold, audacious piece, in that it attacks a still living, but much older (by twenty years), and much more established, writer, the widely respected Catholic novelist, François Mauriac. (Like Sartre, he would go on to win the Nobel Prize in Literature.) And while Sartre had never been a shrinking violet, afraid of engaging in polemics, the severity of his criticism of Mauriac surprised many of his readers, some of whom also saw it as excessive and unfair.

Sartre's main criticism of Mauriac was that he (allegedly) treated his characters as pawns, whose sole function was to serve as instruments for the communication of their creator's worldview, rather than as free beings. The essay ends with the memorable, oft-quoted line: "God is not an artist. Neither is Monsieur Mauriac." (MFMF, 80)

>9. **War Diaries** (written 1939-1940, published posthumously, 1983), trans. Quintin Hoare (Brooklyn, NY: Verso, 2012).

In these diaries, one finds descriptions of Sartre's day-to-day experiences as a conscripted soldier mixed in with his reactions to the various books he was reading at the time and, most significantly, the initial formulations of many of the philosophical ideas that he would later present in *Being and Nothingness*.

>10. **The Imaginary** (1940), trans. Jonathan Webber (New York: Routledge, 2010). It has also been translated by Bernard Frechtman as *The Psychology of Imagination* (New York: Washington Square Press, 1966).

Not to be confused with *Imagination*, published four years earlier, this is the work in which Sartre presented his own phenomenological account of imagination and of "imaginaries" (that is, imagined objects). As discussed in Chapter Three above, Sartre analyzes our ability to imagine in terms of our capacity to "nihilate," or negate, what is given in our perceptual field, and to turn our attention, instead, to what is not currently present in that field. And this capacity, in turn, he regards as evidence of our fundamental freedom.

11. **Being and Nothingness** (1943), trans. Hazel E. Barnes (New York: Washington Square Press, 1992). There is also a translation by Sarah Richmond (New York: Routledge, 2018).

This dense and massive work, exceeding 700 pages in length, is widely considered to be Sartre's greatest philosophical work. Its subtitle is "A Phenomenological Essay on Ontology." Ontology is the study of being, and *Being and Nothingness* attempts to describe the basic categories of being and their interrelations. It must be emphasized, however, that when Sartre speaks of "being," he is usually not talking about entities or substances, but rather the *way* in which something exists. So a phrase such as "the being of consciousness" does not refer to the kind of entity consciousness is, but rather to the various modalities of being conscious.

The book's most fundamental analytical tool is the distinction between "being-in-itself" (the manner of being of things, of objects for consciousness, of unconscious beings) and "being-for-itself" (intentionality, the way of being of consciousness.) The term "for-itself" is apt, since a conscious being is aware of itself, reflects on itself, and thus to that extent stands apart from itself. The being of a rock or a table, by contrast, is in-itself, that is, identical with itself, at no distance from itself, and having no awareness of, or relation to, itself. One piece of evidence that Sartre used these phrases to refer to ways of being, rather than to different kinds of entities, is that in the latter half of the book he introduced the concept of "being-for-others," which is obviously not a different kind of thing or entity. Instead, the modality "being-for-others" is a way of being in which a conscious being is not a *subject*, firing its awareness outward at objects in the world, but rather an *object* of which others are aware.

The major theme of the book is the idea that consciousness is not a thing, but an activity, and that it is largely through its focusing activity that a massive, meaningless plenitude of being is carved up, shaped, articulated, and thus transformed into a meaningful world. As discussed in Chapter Three, this is accomplished by consciousness's achievement in elevating part of its perceptual field to the foreground while pushing other parts of it into an undifferentiated background. This ability to negate, or "nihilate" being, also holds the key to freedom, as discussed in Chapter Four. It is a remarkable fact that Sartre wrote this book, perhaps the most extensive defense of freedom ever written, during World War II, and during a stage of the war when defeat at the hands of the Nazis and fascists seemed a very real possibility.

But perhaps the most extraordinary feature of this work is the fact that it deals so comprehensively with so many of the salient features of human existence: freedom, responsibility, relations with others, work, embodiment, emotion, perception, imagination, death, temporality, desire, anguish, bad faith, and knowledge, among others. There is no other book like it.

12. **The Flies** (1943), trans. Stuart Gilbert, in *No Exit and Three Other Plays* (New York: Viking, 1989).

This was Sartre's first published, and first professionally produced, play. In it, he dramatized some of his ideas about freedom—more specifically, the freedom of the French under Nazi occupation. Since the French were subject to censorship under German rule, Sartre made use of allegory, cleverly setting the action in ancient Greece, and presenting the work as a classical tragedy. The censors, failing to grasp Sartre's meaning, allowed the play to be produced. French audiences suffered from no such difficulties.

13. "**The Outsider Explained**" (1943), in *Critical Essays*. This same translation, though entitled "*The Stranger* Explained," is also included in *We Have Only This Life to Live*. A different translation, titled "A Commentary on *The Stranger*," is included in *Existentialism is a Humanism*, trans. Carol Macomber (New Haven, Connecticut: Yale University Press, 2007). Yet another translation, titled "Camus' *The Outsider*," can be found in *Literary and Philosophical Essays*.

When he wrote this review, Sartre had not yet met Albert Camus. The two would eventually become good friends, only to drift apart over political differences, and then to break fully, and publicly, in the wake of the publication of a harsh review of Camus' *The Rebel* in Sartre's journal, *Les Temps Modernes*. The two men shared much in common. Both were extremely versatile writers, achieving a high level of success in the diverse literary genres of fiction, theater, journalism, and philosophy. Both would go on to win the Nobel Prize in Literature. Both were called "existentialists." And Camus's *The Stranger* was often paired with Sartre's *Nausea* as one of the two great existentialist novels.

While Sartre's review of *The Stranger* was highly favorable, it did underscore a crucial, but often overlooked or misunderstood, difference between Camus's philosophy and his own. This difference concerns the concept of "absurdity," which is the central concept in Camus's philosophy, but not in Sartre's. As Sartre explained it in a 1945 interview, "Camus' philosophy is a philosophy of the absurd, and for him the absurd is born from the relation of man with the world, man's rational expectations and the irrationality of the world.... For me there's no such thing as the absurd in this sense." (ICF, 19)

While Sartre did occasionally speak of "absurdity," his meaning is quite different. Bare existence itself, not focused on in any particular way, and not observed under the color of some set of concepts or categories, is meaningless, and, in that sense, absurd.

Where Sartre differed from Camus, then, was on the issue of whether our lives as lived are absurd, or, to put it another way, whether our experience of the world is absurd. On Sartre's view, it clearly is not. Recall that he credited phenomenology with restoring to the world the rich array of values and meanings that we regularly encounter in our daily experience. In his review of Camus's novel, he offered as examples the experiences of listening to a musical piece and watching a rugby match. Both experiences are charged with meaning from the outset. I do not hear a bunch of discrete, unconnected noises, but rather a melody, and perhaps an evocation of melancholy or joy. And I do not see a flurry of random movements involving several people and a ball, but rather, meaningful, coordinated, purposive activity.

But in Camus's narrative technique, according to Sartre,

> what had once been melodic structure has been transformed into a sum of invariant elements. Supposedly this succession of *movements* is rigorously identical with the *act* considered as a whole. Are we not dealing here with the analytic assumption that any reality is reducible to a sum of elements?.... [Camus has] deliberately omitted giving the facts any meaning.... [H]e pretends to reproduce raw experience,... [but] he slyly filters out all the meaningful links that are also part of the experience. That is what Hume did when he stated that he could find nothing in experience but isolated impressions.... By contrast, contemporary philosophy [I assume that Sartre is referring to phenomenology] has established that meanings are also part of immediate data. (COS, 92)

14. **No Exit** (1944), trans. Stuart Gilbert, in *No Exit and Three Other Plays*. This translation also appears in some anthologies under the title *In Camera*.

This was one of Sartre's most successful plays. It has won numerous prizes and has been translated into several languages. It has been repeatedly filmed, televised, and produced for radio, and continues to be performed regularly all around the world.

It originated from Sartre's attempt to solve a practical problem. He had agreed to write a play for three of his actor friends, when it dawned on him that there would be problems of jealously and resentment if any one of them were to be given more lines or more stage time than the others. Then a solution occurred to him: he would put all of them in the same room together for the entire length of the play, with none of them ever exiting. From this premise, not much of a leap was required in order to hit upon the idea of placing all of them in hell, trapped together for all eternity.

The plot is fairly simple. Each of the three main characters (a man and two women) wants to be assured by at least one of the other two that he or she had been misunderstood, and did not really deserve to be in hell. As the play unfolds, we observe several attempts by each character to receive such assurances from one of the others, only, in every case, to see this effort thwarted, typically because of the words and actions of the third character.

At a certain point in the play, the characters notice that, although they are in hell, no one has come in to torture them. Inez, the most intelligent of the three characters, figures out what is going on: "It's obvious what they're after—an economy of man-power—or devil power, if you prefer. The same idea as in the cafeteria, where customers serve themselves.... I mean that each of us will act as torturer of the two others" (NE, 18). And at the play's climax, Garcin comes to recognize the truth of Inez's analysis: "So this is hell. I'd never have believed it. You remember all we were told about the torture chambers, the fire and brimstone.... Old wives' tales! There's no need for red-hot pokers." Then he utters perhaps the most famous line in all of Sartre's gigantic corpus: "Hell is—other people!" (NE. 46-47)

Since Sartre was an atheist who did not believe in hell, the play is best interpreted as an allegory. And indeed, several of Sartre's philosophical ideas are powerfully dramatized in it. One of these is bad faith. For example, Garcin, who had fled to Mexico when a war broke out, desperately wants to be told that he is not a coward. He makes the argument that he had simply died too young, that he might have done some heroic things if only he had been granted more time in which to do them. He is not so brazen as to insist that he definitely *would* have done heroic deeds, settling for the more modest, and somewhat pathetic, insistence that the issue has been "left in suspense, forever." (NE, 39) His bad faith is further illustrated by his evidentiary double standard, in that he bases his claim that he is not a coward on the principle that a life can't be judged by a single action (NE, 44), having apparently forgotten that he had earlier declared that he would have been happy to judge himself by a single act if it had been a courageous one (NE, 39).

The play also illustrates some aspects of Sartre's analyses of interpersonal human relations, especially that our self-image tends to be based substantially on our sense of how we are seen and judged by others, and that relations among people in bad faith are characterized by unending conflict.

It can also be profitably interpreted as an allegory about Sartre's atheism. The characters in No Exit all seek salvation through the redeeming judgment of others. But such judgment is not forthcoming. Similarly, Sartre seemed to be saying that the hope for a Christ to pay for our sins, and a God to forgive us for them, will also be frustrated. Sartre's atheistic existentialism is thus an extremely demanding worldview. It states that it is important to get things right the first time, since no God is going to set your wrong deeds right. The best you can hope for is that, if you wrong others, they might be persuaded to forgive you. No God is party to the transaction. There is, and can be, "no exit" from our freedom, and from our responsibility for everything we do.

15. **"The Republic of Silence"** (1944), in *The Aftermath of War*, trans. Chris Turner (New York: Seagull Books, 2008). This translation is also included in *We Have Only This Life to Live*.

This is one of Sartre's most widely read essays. Brief, but extremely eloquent, it has often been translated, quoted, and anthologized. Its opening line, the seemingly paradoxical assertion that "we were never more free than under the German occupation," is one of the most famous in all of Sartre's writings. The implications of that line are discussed extensively in Chapter Two.

16. **"A More Precise Characterization of Existentialism"**

(1944), in Michel Contat and Michel Rybalka, eds., *The Writings of Jean-Paul Sartre, Vol. 2: Selected Prose*, trans. Richard McCleary (Evanston, IL: Northwestern University Press, 1985). This same translation, though entitled "Existentialism: A Clarification," is also included in *We Have Only This Life to Live*.

In 1944 "existentialism" was a new and fashionable term. Many people who lacked the time and/or ability to read *Being and Nothingness* were curious as to what this new philosophy was all about. Further, as Sartre's fame and influence grew, he began to be attacked with increasing frequency and intensity. Consequently, he was motivated to make a few attempts at explaining his philosophy in a brief and accessible way, while also responding to his critics. This is his first such effort.

The following passage is representative of Sartre's polemical style. In it, he rebuts the charge that his philosophy is discredited by the fact that it had been influenced, in part, by the thought of a Nazi, Martin Heidegger.

> What do you reproach us for? To begin with, for being inspired by Heidegger, a German and a Nazi philosopher.... [But] Heidegger was a philosopher well before he was a Nazi. His adherence to Hitlerism is to be explained by fear, perhaps ambition, and certainly conformism. Not pretty to look at, I agree; but enough to invalidate your neat reasoning. "Heidegger," you say, "is a member of the National Socialist Party; thus his philosophy must be Nazi." That's not it: Heidegger has no character; there's the truth of the matter. Are you going to have the nerve to conclude from this that his philosophy is an apology for cowardice? Don't you know that sometimes a man does not come up to the level of his works? And are you going to condemn *The Social Contract* because Rousseau abandoned his children? And what difference does Heidegger make anyhow? If we discover our own thinking in that of another philosopher, if we ask him for techniques

and methods that can give us access to new problems, does this mean that we espouse every one of his theories? (MPCE, 155-56)

17. "**Introducing Les Temps modernes**" (1945), trans. Jeffrey Mehlman, in We Have Only This Life to Live.

In this essay, Sartre presented the principles that would guide editorial policy for his new journal, Les Temps modernes. He defended the controversial position that writers, instead of pursuing some timeless conception of literary art, should address, and take a stand on, the major issues of their own time.

18. **Roads of Freedom** (1945-1949). Usually mistranslated as "Roads to Freedom," This multivolume novel consists of three completed volumes and a fourth that was abandoned, unfinished. The first volume is The Age of Reason, trans. Eric Sutton (New York: Vintage, 1992). The second is The Reprieve, trans. Eric Sutton (New York: Vintage, 1992). The original French versions of these two books were published in 1945. The third volume, which might have been translated as "Death in the Soul," has instead been published as Troubled Sleep, trans. Gerard Hopkins (New York: Vintage, 1992), in its American edition, with the same translation being rendered as Iron in the Soul (New York: Penguin, 2002) in the British edition. The original French version of this volume appeared in 1949. The incomplete fourth volume is The Last Chance, trans. Craig Vasey (New York: Continuum, 2009). While a portion of its original French version had been published in 1949, the entire (incomplete) text did not appear until 1981.

While in my opinion, this does not rank among Sartre's most distinguished works, it nonetheless belongs on this list by virtue of its length, and, more significantly, because it is one of just two novels that he wrote (the other being *Nausea*). As its title suggests, the theme of this work is freedom. As Paris was liberated from Nazi occupation, Sartre's central characters also strove, though in most cases less successfully, toward their own liberation. Perhaps the most noteworthy feature of this novel is that it exhibits Sartre's growing interest in the social and political aspects of freedom, complementing his already well-established work on its ontological and psychological dimensions.

> 19. ***Existentialism is a Humanism*** (1946), trans. Carol Macomber (New Haven, Connecticut: Yale University Press, 2007). It has also been translated by Philip Mairet as *Existentialism & Humanism* (London: Methuen, 1973), and by Bernard Frechtman as *Existentialism* (New York: Philosophical Library Library, 1947).

This is the second work of Sartre's that appears on this list for reasons other than my assessment of its merits. It is a slightly modified transcript of an extemporaneous lecture in which Sartre replied to several objections to his philosophy while at the same time attempting to present a simplified version of that philosophy for the benefit of a general audience.

By some measures, the lecture was a smashing success. It was delivered to a standing-room-only audience, and sold 500,000 copies within one month of its publication. It has been widely anthologized, and included in almost every kind of textbook that wants to feature something on existentialism, and now stands as the most widely read lecture of all time.

But in my judgment, it suffers from two grave defects. The first is that it was delivered at a time when Sartre's thought was evidently in a state of transition, since it prominently features several ideas that appear nowhere else in his corpus, neither in his earlier works nor in his later ones. While there is nothing wrong in principle with a philosopher trying out some new ideas in a public lecture, the problem is that his remarks were, understandably, taken as comprising a definitive statement, by the man himself, of the meaning of his dense, lengthy, and technical *Being and Nothingness*.

The second problem is that the lecture is littered with careless errors. For example, as it is nearing its end he defined "existentialism" as "nothing else but an attempt to draw all the conclusions from a consistently atheistic position" (EH, 53,). This is consistent with his stated opposition, presented earlier in the lecture, to those who claim that "nothing will have changed if God does not exist." (EH, 28) But then, right at the lecture's conclusion, in the final paragraph of the printed text, he suddenly, and without explanation, abruptly contradicted himself and affirmed the opposite position: "Existentialism...affirms that even if God were to exist, it would make no difference—that is our point of view" (EH, 53). Similarly, he stated his agreement with a famous quotation from Dostoyevsky, "If God does not exist, everything is permissible," even going so far as to call this the very "starting point of existentialism." (EH, 28-29) But this contradicted his stable, repeatedly articulated opposition to that position. In an entry from his *War Diaries*, written in 1939, six years prior to his delivery of the *Existentialism is a Humanism* lecture, he calls Dostoyevsky's statement "a great error," adding that "whether God exists or does not exist, morality is an affair 'between men' and God has no right to poke his nose in. On the contrary, the existence of morality, far from proving God, keeps him at a distance." (WD, 108) And in an interview conducted in 1951, six years after he had given the lecture, he asserted that the problem of morality "is the same whether God exists or not." In a 1974 conversation with Beauvoir, he maintained the same position, remarking, specifically in opposition to the Dostoyevsky quotation, "I clearly see that killing a man is wrong. Is directly, absolutely wrong...." (A, 439). In these later statements, he makes no mention of the fact that he had said the opposite in *Existentialism is a Humanism*, and thus fails to explain the contradiction.

This is not intended to imply, however, that nothing of value can be found in Sartre's lecture. The problem with it is that it will grossly mislead anyone who assumes it is an accurate summary of Sartre's stable philosophical position, or that it fairly represents his usual standard of philosophical acumen. But read in conjunction with his other works, it contains a wealth of interesting material. Most notably, it is in this lecture that Sartre presented his famous example of the student who must choose between caring for his mother and joining the fight against the Nazis. Also, it contains one of his clearest explanations of why one cannot relieve oneself of responsibility by following directives from others. Finally, it is noteworthy that this lecture explicitly answers the series of questions that Sartre had posed at the conclusion of *Being and Nothingness*. (All three of these points are discussed further in Chapter Two).

20. **The Victors** (1946), in *Three Plays* (New York: Knopf, 1949). It has also been translated by Kitty Black as *Men Without Shadows*, in *Altona and Other Plays* (New York: Penguin, 1960).

This is a rather grim and disturbing play, as befits its subject matter—torture. Set in France during the time of the German occupation, it explores the theme of responsibility—that of the jailors who choose to use torture as an interrogation technique, and that of the resistance fighters who must choose between being tortured and betraying their comrades in the resistance. Sadly, recent events have underscored the relevance of these issues to contemporary Americans.

21. **The Respectful Prostitute** (1946), trans. Lionel Abel in *No Exit and Three Other Plays*. It has also been translated by Kitty Black as *The Respectable Prostitute*, in *Two Plays* (Harmondsworth, Middlesex, England: Penguin, 1965).

Sartre was perhaps the first major white philosopher to express serious moral concern about racism, and to treat it as an important philosophical subject. A case in point is this play, about racism in the United States. Unsurprisingly, the play was a hit in the Soviet Union and in Cuba. Surprisingly, it was also successful in the United States, despite problems with censors in many cities.

This is the only play of Sartre's that is set in the United States. He wrote it following a five-month trip to the United States (January-May, 1945), during which he observed American racism first hand.

Sartre took heat from some quarters, for having had the audacity, as a Frenchman, to criticize the United States. His response (in part): "It was said I was anti-American. I am not anti-American. I don't even know what the word means. I am anti-racist because I know what racism means...." (as quoted in CR, 199).

22. **Anti-Semite and Jew** (1946), trans. George J. Becker (New York: Schocken Books, 1995).

Putting his concept of bad faith to good use, Sartre here offered an analysis of anti-Semitism. One might have thought that the French, having just fought a war against the Nazis, would warmly welcome a book condemning a central evil characteristic of this enemy. But Sartre's main target was *French* anti-Semitism, which had existed long before the advent of Nazism, had continued to flourish during the war against it (many French had been complicit in Hitler's genocidal campaign), and continued to flourish after the war's conclusion, as shown by the widespread French resistance to the prospect of welcoming back those French Jews who had been deported by the Nazis. The urgency of Sartre's project stemmed from his desire to puncture the smug complacency of those in France and other Western democracies who falsely assumed that in defeating Nazism they had also defeated, and shown themselves to be above, prejudice, racism, and hatred.

23. "**Cartesian Freedom**" (1946), in *Critical Essays*. A different translation can be found in *Literary and Philosophical Essays*.

This essay was very helpful in making clear where Sartre agreed, and where he disagreed, with Descartes. Sartre credited his great predecessor in French philosophy with the discovery that freedom is connected to the "negative" powers of consciousness—powers to doubt, to negate, and to deny. Some of Sartre's criticisms of Descartes are discussed in Chapter Three.

24. "**Forgers of Myths**" (1946), in *Sartre on Theater*, trans. Frank Jellinek (New York: Pantheon, 1976).

This widely anthologized essay is the most important statement of Sartre's theory of theater. Whereas he referred to the major plays of the period between the two world wars as "a theater of characters," consisting of "psychological studies of a coward, a liar, an ambitious man or a frustrated one," (FOM, 34) he characterized his own plays, as well as those of Beauvoir and Camus, as "a theater of situations." He elaborated: "our aim is to explore all the situations that are most common to human experience, those which occur at least once in the majority of lives." (FOM, 36) This change in emphasis reflects Sartre's rejection of the view that our pre-established character determines what we will do, and his conviction that the drama in a human life is to be found in one's free and creative responses to the various circumstances that he or she must face—for it is precisely by means of such free choices and actions that one's character is formed.

25. "**Materialism and Revolution**" (1946), in *The Aftermath of War*. A different translation can be found in *Literary and Philosophical Essays*.

This lengthy essay is an important early statement of Sartre's thinking on social, political, and historical questions. It is a polemic, directed not so much against Marx as against the French "orthodox" Marxists of the time. In response to criticisms from these Marxists, Sartre here emphasized his distinction between different senses of freedom, and argued, as discussed in Chapter Four, that only an ontologically free person can be oppressed or stand in need of liberation.

26. ***Baudelaire*** (1947), trans. Martin Turnell (New York: New Directions, 1967).

This book on the 19th-century French poet Charles Baudelaire is distinctive for two reasons. It was Sartre's first book-length biography, and it is his first major attempt at the existential psychoanalysis of a single person. "Existential psychoanalysis," an idea that he had introduced in *Being and Nothingness*, is his name for the endeavor to understand a human life in its totality without resorting to deterministic explanations. Its underlying premise is that there is a decipherable logic to the choices that a given person makes, in that the different choices are connected to one another hierarchically, and flow from a (discoverable) fundamental choice.

27. ***The Chips are Down*** (1947), trans. Louise Varése (Boston: Prime Publishers, 1965).

While several of Sartre's stories and plays have been filmed, the distinction of *The Chips are Down* is that it originated as a film script—Sartre's first attempt at that genre. It also stands as an example of the point that not all of his plays or fictional works express his philosophy. Indeed, he described this film scenario as "just the opposite of an existentialist play." He explains: "My first film, *The Chips are Down*, will not be existentialist.... My script is bathed in determinism, because I thought I was allowed to have fun too." (as quoted in CR, 163-164)

28. "**The Responsibility of the Writer**" (1947), trans. Betty Askwith, in Haskell M. Block and Herman Salinger, eds., *The Creative Vision* (New York: Grove Press, 1960).

This lecture developed several of the ideas on responsibility that are discussed in Chapter Two, including, most notably, that we are as responsible for what we could have done but declined to do, that is, our inactions, as we are for our actions.

29. "**What is Literature?**" (1947), trans. Bernard Frechtman, in *"What is Literature?" and Other Essays* (Cambridge, MA: Harvard University Press, 1988).

This controversial and much-discussed work contains Sartre's most extensive discussion of his views on literary aesthetics. It contains his ideas, discussed in Chapter Two, about the moral and political duties of writers, and about the ways in which the writer-reader relationship exemplifies freedom.

30. *Notebooks for an Ethics* (written 1947-1948, published posthumously, 1983), trans. David Pellauer (Chicago: University of Chicago Press, 1992).

This very substantial volume, at more than 500 pages, presents just a fraction of the fruits of Sartre's abortive project, announced at the very end of *Being and Nothingness*, to work out an ethics. While he is believed to have filled ten notebooks with his thoughts on this topic, only two of them, published posthumously in this text, have as of yet been found.

In addition to the topics discussed in Chapter Two, such as the analysis of generosity, and the sketch of an axiological ethics of freedom, one might also mention the *Notebooks*' very extensive and nuanced discussions of oppression (especially NFE, 325-411), bad

Suggested Reading | 115

faith (NFE, 474-99), and anti-black racism in the United States (NFE, 561-74).

Finally, since Sartre is often interpreted as holding that all human relations ultimately are characterized by conflict and hostility, it is worth quoting from his account of "authentic love" in the *Notebooks*: "Here is an original structure of authentic love...: to unveil the Other's being-within-the-world...; to *rejoice* in it without appropriating it; to give it safety in terms of my freedom, and to surpass it only in the direction of the Other's ends." (NFE, 508)

> 31. **Dirty Hands** (1948), trans. Lionel Abel in *No Exit and Three Other Plays*. It has also been translated by Kitty Black as *Crime Passionnel* (London: Methuen, 1961).

This is one of Sartre's most commercially successful and critically acclaimed plays. Though it is almost universally admired, interpretations of its meaning are wildly divergent. Many conservatives love the play, and see it as delivering a strong anti-communist message. Others think its great strength lies in the powerful and dramatic case it makes for the justifiability of political violence in the pursuit of progressive political ends.

One reason for these differing reactions is that the two main characters in the play, Hoederer and Hugo, are presented equally sympathetically, as are the opposed positions they take on the central issue with which the play deals—the ethics of political violence.

Perhaps the most memorable lines in the play are those delivered by Hoederer in response to Hugo's defense of sticking to moral means in the pursuit of political ends:

> How you cling to your purity, young man! How afraid you are to soil your hands! All right, stay pure! What good will it do? Why did you join us? Purity is an idea for a yogi or a monk. You intellectuals and bourgeois anarchists use it as a pretext for doing nothing. To do nothing, to remain motionless, arms at your sides, wearing kid gloves. Well, I have dirty

hands. Right up to the elbows. I've plunged them in filth and blood. But what do you hope? Do you think you can govern innocently? (DH, 223-24)

These lines are delivered by a communist. So was Sartre saying that communists are ruthless killers? Or did he endorse Hoederer's speech as a sensible rebuke to a naïve, self-indulgent, and ineffectual idealist? The answer is not obvious, and the play leaves audience members with much to ponder and discuss.

32. **In the Mesh** (1948), trans. Mervyn Savill (London: Andrew Dakers, 1954).

Though written as a screenplay, In the Mesh has never been filmed. However, it has been adapted for the stage and performed in Switzerland, Italy, Germany, and France. Like *Dirty Hands*, it deals with the issue of political violence, and more generally, with the moral dilemmas attendant to the relationship between ends and means.

The protagonist, Jean Aguerra, is a revolutionary who has become president of a small oil-producing country (presumably in Central America or in the Caribbean) located in the shadow of a superpower (presumably the United States). Aguerra's party had fought the revolution on a platform calling for three things: the nationalization of the country's oil industry, freedom of speech, and the election of a parliament. However, almost immediately upon taking office Aguerra receives a visit from the ambassador of the neighboring superpower, who warns the new president that any attempt on the property of their nationals will result in war. Thus, despite the fact that he had promised to nationalize the oil wells, and his people expect and want him to do so, he realizes that he cannot immediately do so. His tiny country would have no chance of surviving a war with its mighty neighbor. So his only hope is to stall, waiting for the superpower to be distracted by a war elsewhere before taking any action that might otherwise provoke it. But this decision sets up a chain reaction resulting in a series of other repressive measures. Now Aguerra cannot allow the election of a parliament, for he knows it would immediately nationalize the oil. Nor can he allow freedom of the press, which would stir up public opinion to the point where his government could not survive politically without keeping its promises with regard to oil.

The screenplay has a chilling ending. Aguerra is overthrown. As he is led away to be executed, we are placed in the office of the new president, who had ordered his execution. He is speaking to the same ambassador who had visited Aguerra: "We shall not touch the oil fields." (ITM, 128)

> 33. **"Black Orpheus"** (1948), in *The Aftermath of War*. This translation is included in *We Have Only This Life to Live*. There is also a translation by John MacCombie in *"What is Literature?" and Other Essays*. Finally, it has been published as a stand-alone book, in a translation by S. W. Allen (Paris: French & European Pubns, 1951).

This widely read essay was originally published as the introduction to an anthology of French language poems by black and Malagasy poets.

Addressing white readers, the essay begins with these words:

> When you removed the gag that was keeping these black mouths shut, what were you hoping for? That they would sing your praises? Did you think that when they raised themselves up again, you would read adoration in the eyes of these heads that our fathers had forced to bend down to the very ground? Here are black men standing, looking at us, and I hope that you—like me—will feel the shock of being seen. For three thousand years, the white man has enjoyed the privilege of seeing without being seen.... (BO, 291)

34. **"The Quest for the Absolute"** (1948), in *The Aftermath of War*. This translation is also included in *We Have Only This Life to Live*. A different translation can be found in *Essays in Aesthetics*, trans. Wade Baskin (New York: Washington Square Press, 1966).

This sympathetic, insightful, and beautifully written essay on the sculptures of the great Swiss artist, Alberto Giacometti, ranks as perhaps the best of Sartre's many commentaries on works in the visual arts.

35. **"Consciousness of Self and Knowledge of Self"** (1948), trans. Mary Ellen Lawrence and Nathaniel M. Lawrence, in Nathaniel M. Lawrence and D. J. O'Connor, eds., *Readings in Existential Phenomenology* (Englewood Cliffs, NJ: Prentice-Hall, 1967).

This lecture, addressed to an audience of philosophy professors, summarizes some of the main theses of *Being and Nothingness*. It offers a much more accurate and careful self-interpretation than can be found in the vastly more widely read *Existentialism is a Humanism*. A transcript of the discussion that followed the lecture is included in this publication.

36. ***Truth and Existence*** (written 1948, published posthumously, 1989), trans. Adrian van den Hoven (Chicago: University of Chicago Press, 1992).

This important text addresses the nature of truth, the ethics of belief, and the various strategies of bad faith whereby people achieve ignorance of the truth so as to avoid their responsibility for dealing with it. Some of Sartre's arguments in this work are discussed in Chapter Two.

37. **"The Artist and His Conscience"** (1950), in *Portraits*, trans. Chris Turner (New York: Seagull Books, 2017). A different translation can be found in *Situations*, trans. Benita Eisler (Greenwich, Connecticut: Fawcett Crest, 1965).

Though he wrote almost nothing on the subject, music was very important to Sartre, throughout his life. He enjoyed playing the piano on a daily basis and was an avid listener, and a knowledgeable student of classical music and jazz.

In this interesting but rather inconclusive essay, Sartre wrestled with the problem of explaining how music can be meaningful, and how its quite evident aesthetic value can be explained, given that it is a "non-signifying" art (AHC, 32). Recall that in Sartre's writings on literature he emphasizes its value in disclosing truths about the world. But instrumental music has no words—and yet surely we are not to reject "the sonata, the quartet, and the symphony" as meaningless, pointless, and worthless (AHC, 30). How, then, are we to understand it? Sartre pursues this issue, without resolving it, focusing especially on complex and demanding modernist pieces.

38. **The Devil and the Good Lord** (1951), in *The Devil and the Good Lord and Two Other Plays*, trans. Kitty Black (New York: Vintage, 1960). This same translation, though entitled *Lucifer and the Lord*, is also included in *Two Plays*.

Of all of his dramatic works, this was Sartre's personal favorite. It is an extremely lengthy, complex, and ambitious play, as it requires three acts, eleven scenes, and ten sets, deals simultaneously with a multitude of issues, and lasts more than four hours in performance.

One of the most noteworthy features of the play is its engagement with large-scale social issues. One of Sartre's characters, Nasti, the leader of a peasants' movement, at one point remarks, "When the rich fight the rich, it is the poor who die." (DGL, 11) This concern for the poor, and righteous indignation at the injustice of their treatment by the rich, will feature prominently in Sartre's work for the rest of his career.

Perhaps the most important message of the play is that pure good, in the world as it stands, is an unattainable goal. Good, at least in most cases, will be mixed to some degree with evil. This can happen in several ways, of which I'll mention three: (1) ignorance—because our knowledge is limited, we are likely to do some evil, either instead of or in addition to good, even if we are trying our best to do good; (2) limited power—sometimes we do not have the resources to do good except by using means that also cause some evil; (3) starting point—the world is so full of evil systems (children working in sweatshops, perpetual war, destruction of the environment, the ruthless exploitation of animals, and so forth) that it is impossible to fight all of them at once. To participate in any of them is to take part in evil. But to refuse to participate in any of them would require one to withdraw from the world and live a monkish existence, which, ironically, would leave the world's evils undisturbed.

These observations point to another issue that is featured in this play, the issue of whether, or to what extent, or in what circumstances, violence is morally justified as a means for fighting evil or promoting good. On the one hand, almost everyone understands and agrees that violence is an evil, best avoided if possible. But on the other hand, a principled objection to violence, even when it offers the only hope for overcoming some great evil, such as, for example, slavery, would seem to make sense only if violence were the only evil, or, at any rate, always the greatest evil. As the example of violent resistance to slavery suggests, frequently the alternative to violence is not peace, but rather simply another kind of violence. Thus, Sartre seemed to be arguing in this play that an ethics of absolute nonviolence is an ethics of passivity and contemplation, rather than of action. It is essentially a religious morality, appropriate only for heaven, not for Earth.

39. **Saint Genet** (1952), trans. Bernard Frechtman (Minneapolis: University of Minnesota Press, 2012).

This is a massive biography, exceeding 650 pages in length, of the French writer Jean Genet. The book is unique among Sartre's biographical works. His other major biographies of writers all take as their subject matter giants of the nineteenth century, figures, such as Charles Baudelaire, Stéphane Mallarmé, and Gustave Flaubert, who might be regarded as Sartre's predecessors, equal in status to him with regard to their place in the canon of French literature. Genet, by contrast, was a contemporary of Sartre's, and a younger one, by five years, at that. Moreover, it is highly unusual for the subject of a biography to be far less famous than his biographer, but that is certainly the case with Sartre's biography of Genet.

In one respect, however, Genet definitely exceeded Sartre, and this may be one of the factors that attracted Sartre to the project. Genet held the distinction of being one of the few writers who was more despised and more vilified by "respectable" society, and whose works were more frequently banned or censored, than was the case with Sartre himself.

Sartre offered *Saint Genet* as an example of his method of existential psychoanalysis. He said that his purpose was

> to indicate the limit of psychoanalytical interpretation and Marxist explanation and to demonstrate that freedom alone can account for a person in his totality; to show this freedom at grips with destiny, crushed at first by its mischances, then turning upon them and digesting them little by little;... to learn the choice that a writer makes of himself, of his life and of the meaning of the universe, including even the formal characteristics of his style and composition, even the structure of his images and of the particularity of his tastes; to review in detail the history of his liberation. (SG, 628)

In a 1969 interview, he said of *Saint Genet* that it is "perhaps the book where I have best explained what I mean by freedom." He explained: "For Genet was made a thief, he said, 'I am a thief, and this tiny change was the start of a process whereby he became a poet..." (IOAT, 35) The meaning of freedom, then, is

> that in the end one is always responsible for what is made of one. Even if one can do nothing else besides assume this responsibility. For I believe that a man can always make something out of what is made of him. This is the limit I would today accord to freedom: the small movement which makes of a totally conditioned social being someone who does not render back completely what his conditioning has given him. Which makes of Genet a poet when he had been rigorously conditioned to be a thief. (IOAT, 34-35)

In explaining what is unique about Genet's writings, Sartre pointed out that it is not their subject matter, as homosexuality and criminality had been treated before, but rather the fact that he invited us to view these topics from the inside:

> we "normal" people know delinquents only from the outside, and if we are ever "in a situation" with respect to them, it is as judges or entomologists.... One is willing to allow a repentant culprit to confess his sins, but on condition that he rise above them; the *good* homosexual is weaned away from his vice by remorse and disgust; it is no longer part of him. He was a criminal but no longer is. He speaks of what he was as if he were *Another*, and when we read his confession we feel ourselves absolutely other than the poor wretch he is speaking about.... [Genet, however,] never speaks to us *about* the homosexual, *about* the thief, but always *as* a thief and *as* a homosexual. His voice is one of those that we wanted never to hear.... He invents the homosexual subject. (SG, 630-32)

This is important because, as Sartre pointed out, just as we tend to see the achievements of scientists, inventors, and artistic geniuses, as somehow reflecting on humanity as a whole, so should we, if we are to be consistent, see ourselves in Genet. Though we don't want to, it is a testament to Gent's talents as a writer that he compels us to do so.

40. **Nekrassov** (1955), in *The Devil and the Good Lord and Two Other Plays*, trans. Kitty Black (New York: Vintage, 1960).

This satire stands out as Sartre's only comic play. While the characters are ridiculed, and many of the scenes are played for laughs, the play still puts forth a serious message. In it, Sartre attacks the mainstream press for its blatant pro-capitalist bias, and for fomenting anti-communist hysteria and oppression. *Nekrassov* was written at the time of McCarthyism in the United States, and Sartre was motivated to write it in part because of his concern that France was starting to go the way of the United States in this regard. Naturally, the reaction of the corporate press, owned and controlled by capitalists, was less than enthusiastic.

41. "**Colonialism is a System**" (1956), in *Colonialism and Neocolonialism*, trans. Azzedine Haddour, Steve Brewer, and Terry McWilliams (New York: Routledge, 2001).

In this essay, Sartre expressed his opposition to colonialism and explained his support, which many in France at the time regarded as treasonous, for the cause of the Algerians in their struggle to gain independence from France. He argued that the colonial system exposes capitalism for what it is in its full horror, for when dealing with the colonized abroad, the capitalists see no need to curb their rapacity, or to disguise it under the veneer of politeness that characterizes bourgeois society. Further, he denounced the hypocrisy of the French who, immediately upon achieving their own liberation from the Germans, thought nothing of intensifying their own colonial oppression of the Algerians.

42. **Search For a Method** (1957), trans. Hazel E. Barnes [New York: Vintage, 1968). This same translation has also been published as *The Problem of Method* (London: Methuen, 1964).

The most notable feature of this book is its astonishing modesty. It owes its origins to a request from a Polish journal for an essay on the current state of existentialism. Sartre's reply is surprising. He insisted that Marxism is the philosophy of our time, and that existentialism is a mere "ideology," a "parasitical system living on the margin of Knowledge, which at first it opposed but into which today it seeks to be integrated" (SFM, 8).

At the conclusion of the book he took this modesty to even greater heights, as he projected a future in which his own philosophical contributions will have been superseded and rendered obsolete:

> From the day that Marxist thought will have taken on the human dimension (that is, the existential project) as the foundation of anthropological Knowledge, existentialism will no longer have any reason for being. Absorbed, surpassed and conserved by the totalizing movement of philosophy, it will cease to be a particular inquiry and will become the foundation of all inquiry. The comments which we have made in the course of the present essay are directed–within the modest limit of our capabilities–toward hastening the moment of that dissolution. (SFM, 181)

43. "**A Victory**" (1958), in *Colonialism and Neocolonialism*. This translation is included in *We Have Only This Life to Live*. It is also included, in a different translation, as the "Preface" to Henri Alleg, *The Question*, trans. John Calder (Lincoln: University of Nebraska Press, 2006).

This powerful essay on torture was inspired by the experiences of Henri Alleg, a journalist who had been tortured by French paratroopers. Alleg had been editor-in-chief of the *Alger Républicain*, an anti-colonial daily paper that published Algerian grievances against France. The French authorities finally banned the paper in September 1955 and arrested many of its journalists. Alleg, who had gone into hiding, was arrested by France's 10th Paratrooper Division on June 12, 1957, on suspicion of undermining the power of the state. While in French custody he was tortured for a period of one month, during which his torturers demanded, unsuccessfully, that he reveal the names of those who had sheltered him while he had been in hiding. The methods of torture included electric shocks, burning, and waterboarding.

When the French authorities finally gave up on their attempt to coerce information from him through torture, they sent him to a military hospital and prison. There he composed, and surreptitiously smuggled out, an account of his ordeal, entitled *La Question*, an equivocal term in French, which can mean either a question or the institution of torture. His report was printed in *L'Humanité*, but the French police promptly confiscated copies. When *La Question* was then published as a book, it achieved the distinction of being first the book banned in France since the eighteenth century.

Sartre, wanting to do what he could to publicize Alleg's damning account, wrote an essay about it, "A Victory," which was published in the March 6, 1958 edition of *L'Express*—which the authorities promptly seized. Later that month "A Victory" was published as a stand-alone pamphlet. The government immediately confiscated and destroyed all copies. Eventually, the authorities relented, and a volume combining Alleg's account with Sartre's essay on it (presented as a preface) was published without governmental interference.

One can understand why the French government did not like Sartre's essay. He points out how the French attitude toward torture had changed significantly in the short period of time separating the present Algerian conflict from the time of the German occupation, when the Gestapo had used torture in an attempt to suppress the Resistance:

> [We] watched the German soldiers walking inoffensively down the street, and would say to ourselves: 'They look like us. How can they act as they do?' And we were proud of ourselves for not understanding.
>
> Today we know that there was nothing to understand.... Now when we raise our heads and look into the mirror we see an unfamiliar and hideous reflection: ourselves.
>
> Appalled, the French are discovering this terrible truth: that if nothing can protect a nation against itself, neither its traditions nor its loyalties nor its laws, and if fifteen years are enough to transform victims into executioners, then its behavior is no more than a matter of opportunity and occasion. Anybody, at any time, may equally find himself victim or executioner.
>
> Happy are those who died without ever having had to ask themselves: 'If they tear out my fingernails, will I talk?' But even happier are others, barely out of their childhood, who have not had to ask themselves that *other* question: 'If my friends, fellow soldiers, and leaders tear out an enemy's fingernails in my presence, what will I do?' (AV, xxviii)

Sadly, as the ongoing American "war on terror" makes clear, Sartre's essay is as relevant today as it was 60 years ago when he wrote it.

44. The Condemned of Altona (1959), trans. Sylvia and George Leeson (New York: Norton, 1978). This same translation has also been published as *Loser Wins* (London: Hamish Hamilton, 1960), and as *Altona*, in *Altona and Other Plays*.

This was Sartre's last major play, and it is generally thought to be one of his best. Set in post–World War II Germany, it can be read, on one level, as a dramatic meditation on German collective guilt over the Holocaust. While the major characters had not been enthusiastic, believing Nazis, they had, like millions of other Germans, cooperated with and assisted the Nazis when it was in their self-interest to do so. Now, when confronted with the facts of history, they offer, both to others and to themselves, feeble rationalizations for their actions. For example, when Gerlach, a wealthy shipping tycoon, is challenged by his son, Franz, to explain why he had sold land to the Nazis, even though he had known that it would be used for a concentration camp, he replies as follows; "What is there to explain? Himmler wanted somewhere to house his prisoners. If I had refused my land, he would have bought some elsewhere.... A little farther to the west, a little farther to the east, the same prisoners would suffer the same guards, and I would have made enemies inside the Government." (ALT, 40)

The Condemned of Altona attempts to make sense of something seemingly inexplicable: how could the unimaginable horrors and atrocities of the twentieth century have happened? The play suggests that attributing them to the century's great monsters, such as Hitler and Stalin, is a shallow explanation, since these villains could not have accomplished what they did without the cooperation of millions. While Hitler and Stalin may have been evil, it was their millions of faceless accomplices who facilitated their crimes, and in so doing justified their actions to themselves with bad-faith rationalizations. For example, some Germans may have said to themselves, "you can't blame me for Hitler's crimes. I didn't approve of his mad schemes. I hated Hitler!" But Franz, who had been a soldier in Hitler's army, rebuts such reasoning, as he says to his father, "We hated Hitler, others loved him. What's the difference? You supplied him with warships, and I with corpses. Tell me, could we have done more if we worshipped him?" (ALT, 36-37)

The moral of the play, I would suggest, is that the cause of the greatest evils is typically not sheer naked malevolence, which is relatively rare, but rather greed, cowardice, conformity, passivity, opportunism, and mindless obedience—which are all too common.

45. ***Critique of Dialectical Reason*** (1960), trans. Alan Sheridan-Smith (New York: Verso, 2004).

This gigantic work ranks, with *Being and Nothingness* (which it exceeds in length by about 140,000 words), as one of Sartre's two most important contributions to philosophy. It works out in greater detail some of the themes concerning the melding of existentialism and Marxism that he had first sketched in *Search for a Method*.

The *Critique* differs from *Being and Nothingness* in its subject matter and emphases in at least three respects. (1) Whereas in the earlier book the discussion of interpersonal human relationships had been confined to dyadic and triadic encounters, the *Critique* extensively analyzes large-scale collaborative organizations, such as soccer teams and revolutionary political groups. (2) In the moral sphere, the *Critique* is not so much concerned with the issues of personal authenticity and salvation, which had occupied him in his early works, as with broad problems of social injustice. These two new interests intersect, since, as Sartre went on to argue in the *Critique*, social injustice can only be eliminated or significantly reduced through coordinated group activity. (3) While in *Being and Nothingness* he had certainly acknowledged, and analyzed at length, the fact that freedom perpetually confronts obstacles, and that these obstacles often arise directly as a result of prior acts of freedom, in the *Critique* he pursued this theme on a much larger scale. Free human activity creates vast historical structures and processes, and these, in turn, act on human beings, often in such a way as to diminish their freedom (in the sense of "freedom of obtaining," discussed in Chapter Four). To put it succinctly, we make history; and then history makes us. In this way, Sartre connected his account of freedom with the analysis of alienated labor that Marx presents in *The Economic and Philosophic Manuscripts of 1844*.

In his account of alienated freedom, Sartre introduced two new concepts: "practico-inert" and "counter-finality." The former term refers to the tendency of human creations, or even of natural, pre-existing things that humans have worked on and altered, to restrict our freedom in the future. We freely create (or modify) objects, systems, conventions, and large-scale societal structures, often for the very reason that they will enhance our freedom in some way—and they typically do, at least in the short run. But the meanings that we thereby create tend to ossify, and thus resist our future attempts to alter them, or to escape from them, through subsequent free actions. A vacant plot of ground might be put to a thousand different purposes, but once one has been chosen, and acted upon (let us say that a parking lot has been constructed), it is then much more difficult even to envision, let alone bring to reality, any other possible meaning and use for it (such as the creation of a green public park, complete with fields for soccer and baseball). One of the possible meanings of this plot of ground, lent to it by means of free human practice, has now become "inert," stable, and resistant to change.

The concept of "counter-finality" refers to an even more radical way in which my freedom, having become encrusted in things, can come back to restrict my freedom. Whereas the practico-inert tendency of things would appear to be an inevitable consequence of human freedom, following from the simple point that in choosing one alternative one necessarily closes off others, a counter-finality actually "opposes the process which produces it" (CDR, 193). Sartre offered the example of the deforestation of China's mountainsides and hillsides by Chinese peasants. They had done this in an effort to increase the amount of available farmland. But the unintended result was massive flooding, resulting in the erosion of the land they already had.

The *Critique* offers a similar analysis of several other traditions, institutions, technologies, family structures, economic arrangements, and other kinds of complex human creations that can condition and frustrate human freedom. Each of these structures facilitates some further choices, just as it also stands as an obstacle to others. There is thus established a dialectical relation between persons and their environment (and their history). In describing this relation, Sartre argued both that agents "interiorize" these historical, societal, economic, and environmental structures (the structures act on us through the mediation of interpretation and understanding, rather than by means of mechanistic causality); and that our free actions, in turn, project out into the world, modifying it, and thus becoming "exteriorized" in it, as part of the practico-inert.

This relates to another central concept of the *Critique*, the "progressive-regressive" method for understanding a person. The regressive part deals with the social and historical background against which the person acts. The progressive part deals with the person's aims and goals—how he or she freely and creatively responds to this background. In this light, one might characterize the relationship of the *Critique* to Marxism this way: Sartre proposed to give full weight to Marxist insights on class, on historical conditioning, and on the force of economic structures, without going so far as to endorse historical determinism. Or, to put it more positively, his project is to synthesize these Marxist insights with his own discoveries concerning individual freedom and responsibility.

Sartre's insistence on individual freedom leads to one more important disagreement with the Marxism of the French Communist Party—over the cardinal Marxist concept, that of class. To make this disagreement clear, it is necessary to say something about another pair of concepts that play a central role in the *Critique*: "series" and "group." A "series," according to Sartre's distinction, is an unstructured and uncoordinated social collective. It is a collection of people who share something in common, on the basis of which they also have in common the same individual purpose, even though they do not share a common purpose. Sartre's example is that of a line of people waiting to board a bus (CDR, 256-69). Each person in the line wants a seat on the bus, but may not care about the fact that each other person also wants a seat. Thus, each member of the line is to each of the others either superfluous (if there will be enough seats on the bus to accommodate all of them) or an obstacle (if there will not be). Even though the members of this loose collective may not know, or care about, each other, they are still capable of bringing about a certain minimum amount of cooperative organization—that of forming a line and then waiting peacefully in it before boarding the bus in turn, and in an orderly manner. They undertake this cooperative activity, which involves the minor inconvenience of having to defer to those ahead of oneself in line, because they recognize that the alternative, that of fighting each other for a seat, would be much worse.

In contrast to a series, which is incapable of achieving any intended result significantly more impressive than that of standing peacefully in a bus queue, a "group" is capable of major accomplishments. The difference between a series and a group is that the individuals in the latter *do* share a collective purpose. The individual members of a group band together in common cause, self-consciously adopt each other's goals as their own, and work together, in a complex coordination of efforts, to achieve them. Examples of "groups" in this technical sense would be a soccer team, a musical ensemble, and a revolutionary political organization. In a departure from the individualism of *Being and Nothingness*, in the *Critique* Sartre argued that it is primarily groups, rather than individuals acting alone, that make history.

This brings us back to Sartre's disagreement with the French Communist Party, which had often asserted that the working class can be counted on to act collaboratively in favor of actions or policies that advance the interests of the individual members of that class. But that, in Sartre's view, conflates the distinction between a series and a group. The working class, like the people standing in a bus queue, are members of a series—by virtue of their sharing in common certain objective circumstances, there are also certain interests that can be ascribed to each of them. But they are not a group. Groups can only be formed as a result of the free choice of individuals to join together in common cause—a choice that can be *motivated* by the economic and political constraints that they, in common with one another, must confront, but not *caused* by them. Indeed, one of the chief obstacles to progress in the political realm is the widespread reluctance of members of any given series to band together as a group for the purpose of concerted action. Moreover, even when members of a series, such as the working class, do freely consent to join a group, there is always the danger that many of them will subsequently exercise their freedom by withdrawing from the group (which often happens either when a battle has been won, with the result that the immediate impetus for forming the group has been withdrawn, or when a protracted battle has not been won, and some abandon the cause because of fatigue and/or despair). There is always the danger that a group will gradually dissolve into impotent seriality. Thus, while Sartre agreed with the orthodox Marxists that the significant political actors upon whom progress depends are groups, rather than individuals, the free choice of the individual retains, for him, its immense importance, since it is only by means of such individual choice that groups can be formed in the first place, and then sustained.

The final major theme of the *Critique* that I will mention is that of scarcity, and its relation to violence. According to Sartre, the major obstacle to human freedom (in the sense of "freedom of obtaining") is material scarcity, that is, the lack of resources (food, drink, clothing, shelter from the elements, and so forth) necessary to meet one's fundamental needs. No one would freely choose to exhaust his or her life in a desperate struggle for bare survival if other options were available. So the content of many workers' lives counts as evidence of their practical unfreedom. Moreover, a life spent in constant struggle for the bare essentials of organic existence leaves little time or energy available for carrying out other freely chosen projects, and in particular those that would have allowed one to exercise his or her distinctively human faculties, such as intellect, imagination, moral sense, creativity, and aesthetic sensibility. Instead of being able to find in one's life room for engaging in such projects as creating and appreciating art, pursuing close personal relationships, engaging with others in critical discussion and in political action, pursuing knowledge, and so forth, one is forced by economic necessity to live the life of an animal. (On this point Sartre's thought was at one with that of the early Marx.)

Sartre then made the argument that the major factor leading to violence, both in the past and in the present, is material scarcity, and the consciousness of such scarcity. This does not mean that everything that happens does so directly by violence. But Sartre did claim that everything takes place *in an atmosphere* of violence, which is also an atmosphere of "interiorized" material scarcity.

In order to grasp his point, one must add that scarcity is no longer imposed on us by nature. There is enough to go around, and no technological barrier to a distribution of the world's resources that would provide enough for everyone. But we persist in social patterns that are left over from the interiorization of past material scarcity. This point is crucial to the understanding of Sartre's political radicalism. It is fueled by his insistence that we are free. The existing social, political, and economic arrangements that enslave and immiserate us are our free creations. They are not imposed on us by nature. Our freedom means that we are not stuck with them, but rather are free to change them. And we should.

46. **"The Wretched of the Earth"** (1961), in *Colonialism and Neocolonialism*. This translation is also available in *We Have Only This Life to Live*. A different translation, entitled "After Colonialism," is included in *Modern Times: Selected Non-Fiction*, trans. Robin Buss (New York: Penguin, 2000).

This essay is one of the most controversial in Sartre's voluminous body of work. It was almost universally loathed in Europe and the United States, but widely celebrated in Africa and Latin America. The essay was originally published as the preface to *The Wretched of the Earth*, a book by Frantz Fanon, the now-famous Martinican psychiatrist, philosopher, and anti-colonial theoretician. While much of Fanon's book is devoted to the topic of the psychiatric effects of colonization, its most controversial aspect is its defense of violence on the part of the colonized in their struggle for liberation from colonization. The outraged reaction to Sartre's preface was based on the fact that in it he enthusiastically, and powerfully, supports Fanon on this point. Indeed, perhaps the most despised passage in Sartre's entire corpus is to be found in this essay. Speaking of the colonists engaged in the struggle to free themselves from European colonization, Sartre wrote: "At the first stage of the revolt, they have to kill: to shoot down a European is to kill two birds with one stone, doing away with oppressor and oppressed at the same time: what remains is a dead man and a free man." (WOTE, 148)

Anticipating the response such a remark will provoke from the defenders of principled nonviolence, Sartre bared his teeth:

> Let us look at ourselves, if we have the courage, and see what is happening to us.
>
> We must first face up to that unexpected spectacle: the strip-tease of our humanism. Here it is, completely naked and not beautiful: it was nothing but an illusory ideology, the exquisite justification for pillage; its tenderness and its affectation sanctioned our acts of aggression. The non-violent are looking pleased with themselves: neither victims nor executioners! Come on! If you are not victims, since the government for which you voted, since the Army in which your young brothers have served, carried out a 'genocide' without hesitation or remorse, then you are unquestionably executioners.... Understand this for once: if the violence had started this evening, if exploitation or oppression had never existed on earth, perhaps this display of non-violence could settle the dispute. But if the entire regime and even your non-violent thoughts are a condition born of an age-old oppression, your passivity only serves to place you on the side of the oppressors (WOTE, 150-51).

47. **Words** (1964), trans. Irene Clephane (Harmondsworth, Middlesex, England: Penguin, 1967). It has also been translated by Bernard Frechtman as *The Words* (New York: Vintage, 1981).

This is Sartre's autobiography, which is devoted almost exclusively to his childhood. It has received nearly universal acclaim, in part because it is beautifully written, but also, one speculates, because it is relatively devoid of inflammatory political statements. As discussed in Chapter One, Sartre here claims that two main interests have dominated his life: reading and writing (hence the appropriateness of the book's title). It was largely in response to this book that Sartre was awarded (though he famously rejected it) the Nobel Prize in Literature.

48. "**Russell Vietnam War Tribunal Inaugural Statement**" (1967), trans. either Richard Miller or Judith Duffett, in We Have Only This Life to Live.

This is the speech that Sartre delivered at the beginning of the tribunal's first meeting, held on May 2, 1967. (Details about the tribunal, and Sartre's involvement in it, are provided in Chapter One.) Sartre, in explaining the rationale for such a tribunal, appeals to the precedent set in Nuremberg, at the conclusion of World War II, when the Nazis were prosecuted for aggression and for war crimes. He notes that no other such tribunals had been instituted in the intervening years, and asked why this is so:

> Are we then so pure? Have there been no war crimes since 1945? Have we never again resorted to violence or to aggression? Have there been no more "genocides"? Has no large country ever tried to destroy by force the sovereignty of a smaller one? Has there never been reason in the entire world for denouncing more Oradours or Auschwitzes? You know the truth: in the last twenty years, the great historical fact has been the struggle of the Third World for its freedoms. The colonial empires have crumbled, and in their place sovereign nations have arisen or have reclaimed their previous and traditional independence which had been destroyed by colonialism. All this has happened amidst suf-

fering, sweat and blood. A tribunal such as that of Nuremberg has become a permanent necessity. (RVWC, 434-35)

49. **On Genocide** (1967), trans. uncredited (Boston: Beacon Press, 1968). It is also included, though entitled "Vietnam: Imperialism and Genocide," in *Between Existentialism and Marxism*, trans. John Mathews (New York: Pantheon, 1974).

The members of the tribunal voted unanimously to adopt Sartre's text, *On Genocide*. Though he had to write it quickly, following the presentation of evidence but prior to the tribunal's final session, he nonetheless succeeded in crafting a powerful document. The following is a sample:

> In October, 1966, General Westmoreland defined [one of the American military objectives] in these terms: "We are making war in Vietnam to show that guerrilla warfare does not pay." To show whom? The Vietnamese? That would be very surprising. Must so many human lives and so much money be wasted merely to teach a lesson to a nation of poor peasants thousands of miles from San Francisco?.... It is to the others that the Americans want to prove that guerrilla warfare does not pay: they want to show all the oppressed and exploited nations that might be tempted to shake off the American yoke by launching a people's war, at first against their own pseudo-governments, the compradors and the army, then against the United States Special Forces, and finally against the GIs. In short, they want to show Latin America first of all, and more generally, all of the Third World. To Che Guevara, who said, "We need several Vietnams," the American government replies, 'They will all be crushed the way we are crushing this one."
>
> In other words, this war is primarily a warning for three, and perhaps four, continents.... So, this exemplary geno-

cide is a warning to all humanity. It is with this warning that six percent of mankind hope, without too much expense, to control the remaining ninety-four percent.... (OG, 70-71)

50. **The Family Idiot** (1971-1972). The original French version was published in three volumes, with the first two appearing in 1971, and the third the following year. The English translation, by Carole Cosman, has been split into five volumes, each published in Chicago by the University of Chicago Press, and appearing in 1981, 1987, 1989, 1991, and 1994.

This biography of Gustave Flaubert (another exercise in existential psychoanalysis) was Sartre's final major work, and by far his longest. Despite its gargantuan size, it remains incomplete, as the projected fourth volume was abandoned, unfinished, as a result of Sartre's blindness.

It is distinctive in that it integrates, all in one work, many of Sartre's most important ideas, drawn from all phases of his career. It deals extensively with the imagination, the subject of his earliest philosophical book, incorporates several concepts from *Being and Nothingness*, makes full use of the progressive-regressive method that he had developed in the *Critique*, and further extends his novel appropriations of Marxist and psychoanalytic themes.

About the Author

David Detmer is Professor of Philosophy at Purdue University Northwest. His many books include *Phenomenology Explained* (2013), *Sartre Explained* (2008), *Challenging Postmodernism* (2003), and *Freedom as a Value* (1988), which received a Choice "Outstanding Academic Titles" award in philosophy. Detmer has also written articles and book chapters on such topics as vegetarianism, the Beatles, the death penalty, Woody Allen, U.S. foreign policy, and modern art. He is a past president of the North American Sartre Society, and for eleven years was executive editor of the journal *Sartre Studies International*.

A Word from the Publisher

Thank you for reading *Simply Sartre*!

If you enjoyed reading it, we would be grateful if you could help others discover and enjoy it too.

Please review it with your favorite book provider such as Amazon, BN, Kobo, Apple Books, or Goodreads, among others.

Again, thank you for your support and we look forward to offering you more great reads.